Introduction

Congratulations on selecting Vagus Nerve: guide to understand how vagus nerve determines psychological and emotional states such as anxiety, depression, migraines, back pain, and simple exercises to improve your life. Thank you for doing so!

The Vagus nerve is an incredible part of your body. It is long, meandering, and powerful. It is unique and complex. It is truly amazing! Sometimes called CNX, this is the tenth cranial nerve, and it extends from the base of your skull to your colon. Along the way down from your brain stem, the Vagus nerve makes several stops along the way, extending in various areas, and acting as an information "highway" for your body to tell the brain what it is experiencing, and for the brain to tell the body how to respond. And in many instances, this is all happening subconsciously!

So how does something that happens without you thinking about it become balanced along the way? Thankfully there are several ways. You can meditate, workout, get a massage, and more. And you can help others stimulate and regulate this nerve as well. For such a vital nerve, it is amazingly easy to stimulate.

But why do you want to stimulate your Vagus nerve and make sure it is functioning properly? Because otherwise, your body is in complete disarray! This nerve is important in the body functions like digestion, breathing, heartbeat, eating, swallowing, talking, seeing clearly, and more. If it is not working, not much else is working properly either.

It is time to learn more about this critical part of your body, how it impacts a variety of functions, and what you can do about it.

There are plenty of books on this subject on the market, thanks again for choosing this one! Every effort was made to ensure it is full of as much useful information as possible, please enjoy!

Chapter 1: What is the Vagus Nerve?

Did you know that the human body has 12 cranial nerves? Did you know that each "nerve" is actually comprised of two nerves, typically left and right nerve intertwined to make the "one" cranial nerve. And these nerves are the link between your body and the brain? Have you ever wondered how the brain and body "talk" to one another? It is all through these cranial nerves. Some of the nerves are responsible for sharing sensory information, like how something sounds or what it tastes like. This means these nerves need to have the sensory function to interpret the smell of something. But then there are other nerves that "talk" with the muscles and even some glands. These nerves are called "motor functions." And finally, while most have a single function, either sensory or muscle, there are others that operate with both. The Vagus nerve is one such nerve.

To help you understand where a nerve is located, each cranial number is assigned a number represented in Roman numerals, for example, I is one, II is two, etc. The Vagus nerve is the tenth nerve and is called CNX, or Cranial Nerve Ten.

In Latin, the word "vagus" is defined as "wandering." When you understand a bit more of the makeup of this nerve, you will realize that this description is pretty accurate. The Vagus nerve is the longest in the human body, and it does a lot of traveling around and through it. Basically, it moves from the base of your skull to your lower torso. You will learn more about the passage of this nerve later in this chapter.

There are two parts to the sensory functions of this particular nerve:

1. **Visceral**: This is used to describe the "feelings," or sensations, in your body's organs.
2. **Somatic**: This term is applied to your physical "feelings," or sensations in the muscles and skin of your body.

Each part of the sensory function is unique. The somatic function gives information regarding the skin from behind the ears. It also shares this information from the ear canal and various parts of the throat. It is also responsible for the visceral information shared to the brain regarding the majority of your digestive tract, heart, lungs, trachea, esophagus, and larynx. Finally, while it is not the primary "player" in the sensations in your tongue, your Vagus nerve does have a small role in how your tongue's root experiences the sensation of taste.

There are three primary motor functions that the Vagus nerve functions with:

1. Stimulates digestion and the digestive tract. This involves involuntary contractions in the majority of your intestines, stomach, and esophagus to help food move through the system.
2. Stimulates your heart. The primary goal is to massage the muscles of the heart in an effort to lower your resting heart rate.
3. Stimulates your mouth. This stimulation includes the soft palate, or the soft area in the back of the roof of your mouth, larynx, and pharynx.

As you can see, this nerve is a fairly powerful player in not just how you feel, but how you experience the world you are living in. It impacts everything from your brain to your digestion, and so much in between. This means if something "goes wrong," it can have dire consequences to your health and well-being. To check to see if it is in working order, many physicians will first begin with your gag reflex. It is often done with a cotton swab, where the doctor "tickles" both sides in your back throat. This causes most people to involuntarily gag. If not, there may be something wrong with this nerve.

Some of the common problems that occur for your Vagus nerve include:

- Nerve damage
- Gastroparesis
- Vasovagal syncope

Nerve Damage

Because of the extreme length and vast scope of this nerve, there can be a variety of symptoms indicating it has been damaged. Most of the time the symptom of Vagus nerve damage depends on the location of the damage. Some of the common symptoms include:

- Stomach acid production is decreased
- Blood pressure is abnormal
- Heart rate is unusual
- Ear pain
- Gag reflux is minimal or lost

- Drinking liquids proves to be a problem
- Wheezy or hoarse voice often
- Loss of voice or challenge speaking
- Vomiting or nausea
- Pain or bloating in the abdomen

Gastroparesis

Gastroparesis is another condition that many experts believe is the result of a damaged Vagus nerve. This concerns the contractions of the digestive tract. When the involuntary contractions are not functioning properly the stomach cannot empty properly. It is a common side effect of vagotomy. This is a procedure that removes some or all of the Vagus nerve. Side effects common to gastroparesis include:

- Blood sugar fluctuations
- Weight loss that is unexplained
- Bloating or bleeding in the abdomen
- Acid reflux
- Feeling full at the beginning of a meal or not having an appetite
- Vomiting or nausea, especially if the vomit contains food that is not digested even hours after eating

Vasovagal Syncope

During stressful situations, the Vagus nerve can overreact. When this happens it can dramatically drop your blood pressure and heart rate, because it is responsible for stimulating the various muscles in your heart to slow down the heart rate. This sudden drop can lead to fainting. Some common stressful triggers include:

- Standing for long periods of time
- The intense strain on the body, including while trying to have a bowel movement
- Having blood drawn or seeing blood
- The concern of harm to the body
- Extreme heat and overexposure

Stimulation to the Vagus Nerve

Currently, not many illnesses are treated with stimulation of the Vagus nerve. Two such illnesses include depression and epilepsy. It is thought that in the future more illnesses can and will be treated with this method, including multiple sclerosis. To stimulate the Vagus nerve, a device is placed inside the body that emits electrical impulses consistently. This stimulates the nerve. Typically this is placed in the chest under the skin, with a wire connecting to the left side of the Vagus nerve. When the device is activated, a signal is sent along the Vagus nerve to the brainstem. This stimulation then communicates to the brain. Typically a neurologist programs the device; however, after that, the person is given a magnet that they can hold in their hand and control the device on their own.

This critical nerve, interfacing with the parasympathetic control of the digestive tract, lungs, and heart, is called CNX. This means that it is the tenth cranial nerve. It used to be referred to as the pneumogastric nerve. While there are typically a pair of nerves making up the Vagus nerve, it is usually referred to as a singular nerve. In the human body, the Vagus nerve makes up the longest autonomic nervous system nerve. The spinal accessory nucleus is the concluding section of the Vagus nerve.

Nestled in between the inferior cerebellar peduncle and the pyramid the Vagus nerve extends, passing through the medulla oblongata, through the jugular foramen, and then enters the carotid sheath, which is located in between the internal jugular vein and the internal carotid artery. It leaves this interior space to travel down the neck and chest, into the abdomen. Once there the Vagus nerve adds to the viscera's innervation, thus extending all the way into the colon. When the two nerve sides, the left and right Vagus nerve, comes through the cranial vault it juts through the jugular foramina and slices through the carotid sheath. It wiggles between the external and internal carotid arteries and then goes through the posterolateral to meet the common carotid artery.

The passage of the Vagus nerve through the body offers some output to a variety of different organs; however, it is primarily designed to share sensory information. In fact, the Vagus nerve makes up almost 90% of the human body's afferent nerves. It shares the information of different organs with the central nervous system. Situated bilaterally, housed inside the Vagus nerve's inferior ganglion, or nodose ganglia, are the cell bodies of visceral afferent fibers.

The right side of the Vagus nerve is the start of the right recurrent laryngeal nerve. This loops around the subclavian artery on the right and heads down in the neck, crossing between the esophagus and the trachea. The right Vagus nerve then keeps going down, passing over the right subclavian anterior artery. It passes posterior to the superior vena cava and then travels down posterior to the primary bronchus on the right. This right Vagus nerve adds to the esophageal, pulmonary, and cardiac plexuses. This important nerve creates the posterior vagal trunk, housed at the bottom of the esophagus. It begins its descent through the diaphragm through the esophageal hiatus.

The left side of the Vagus nerve has a different, but a parallel trajectory. It passes through the thorax, slicing through the left subclavian artery and the left common carotid artery. It then goes into the aortic arch. This develops the left recurrent laryngeal nerve. From here it loops around the aortic arch and moves to the left side of the ligamentum arteriosum. Like the right side of the Vagus nerve, it moves from here through the esophagus and trachea. Unlike the right, the left side of the Vagus nerve sprouts off thoracic cardiac branches. It also disassembles the pulmonary plexus before going inside the esophageal plexus. It finally migrates into the abdomen as part of the anterior vagal trunk as part of the diaphragm's esophageal hiatus.

Chapter 2: The Interchange of Emotional and Psychological States of Being

Currently, the psychological state of modern humanity is not positive. There is a consistent rise in anxiety, depression, and stress. And even more troubling is the psychological distress is affecting younger ages, including teenagers and even young children. Many factors contribute to this increase in mental and emotional destabilization; however, it can probably be related to the confusion about the truth of human condition, misprescribed medication for emotional states, increases in isolation and social loneliness levels, constantly and quickly changing society, and faced-paced lifestyles.

But perhaps the most challenging part of this all is the confusion people have around the fundamental basis of negative emotions and the lack of "training" on how to process those emotions. It is not just about identifying a negative emotion, but also about how to adapt and relate to those emotions while processing the message that it sends. The purpose of this chapter is designed to define emotions, a framework for placing these emotions into a consciousness matrix, describe the process for maladaptive processing and adaptive emotional processing, in addition to suggestions for how to be more adaptive in the future.

Emotions

Emotions are a section of the "core consciousness" system or the experiential system. There are three wide-spread areas for the experiential system, all centered around the "theater" of experience, which ultimately shapes your behavior. The first part is how you experience the world using your senses. For example, you see a house, hear a car horn, smell popcorn. The second is what drives you. For example, when you know something is "bad," you instinctively want to avoid it. Alternatively, when you know something is "good," you want it or more of it. The final area involves your emotions. These are developed as a response to your drivers and experiences. Your emotions are meant to encourage action and prepare you to deal with those situations. For example, think of a cat that is searching for a mouse outside. While hunting, it has a sensory experience when it smells a dog nearby. This triggers a driver to "avoid" the dog because they are "bad" for the cat. The cat will probably freeze to prevent the threat from noticing them, and if the cat then senses that there is no immediate danger, it will move to a new location, away from the dog scent. When the cat no longer senses the dog's presence the fear it felt will go away. This example shows how the emotion of fear created the energy to avoid the dog. Emotions are tied to something, making it a response "set." When your goals or needs change, or you perceive a change, your emotions are activated.

Of course, there are differences from person to person. The temperament and emotional response can vary greatly depending on the individual. Some people, and even animals, have a more sensitive emotional response trigger, offering an intense reaction or having a hard time to "calm down" after being triggered. This is why one situation will always set someone "off," while the same situation never seems to bother someone else.

Yet, while emotions are something we all deal with and respond with, not everyone truly understands them. The current education system in the United States does not offer a developed curriculum regarding mental and emotional health. But emotions are something all adults should be well educated on. The challenge is that human consciousness is a complex and dimensional aspect of your life. If human brains worked like mice brains, for example, the first part of this chapter would suffice. However, there is a dimension of the human consciousness that mice do not appear to have; self-consciousness. This makes things a whole lot more complicated! Self-consciousness is a reaction and response mostly to experiential events. For instance, when the cat feels fear, it simply fears and reacts instinctively. But when a human feels fear, they can first recognize the feeling and then make a judgment about it. Humans can also decide if they want to acknowledge that feeling, and adjust how much or little they feel of it. In addition, when the cat feels fear, it does not care nor recognize that others around it can see it is afraid. They do not notice other cats or beings around them witnessing their response to their fear. Humans can. This is called the "public self-consciousness system." Humans can recognize that others can see their response to a situation if they show a reaction. In addition, humans can think about how other people will respond to their emotional reactions. As a human, you possess various "streams" of consciousness which allow you to process different emotions. This can become very complicated and conflicting.

As an example, think about a parent responding to a child's injury. If the child is crying and expressing their emotions to a situation, the parent can choose how to handle this situation with support or rejection of that display of emotion. This sets the tone for how the child will express their emotions in the future. And, as the child grows, it also sets the tone for how that child secretly "judges" their feelings and emotions when they are older. This example is also a good representation of the three different types of human consciousness; the experiential self, private self, and public self. The public self is the way you choose to show yourself to other people, while the private self is how you internally judge or explain your core emotions. Third, the experiential self is the house for your core feelings. The relationship between all of these is complicated and powerful.

Adaptive and Maladaptive

Now that you have the foundational understanding of how your consciousness works, you are ready to explore the process of experiencing emotions. This is why some people "process" or "handle" their emotions one way instead of another. Some processing is productive and "good" for you, while there are other "coping strategies" for emotions that are not as helpful. These "other" strategies are called "maladaptive." In the example above regarding an adult's response to an emotional child, there can sometimes be discord between public emotional display or the private self and one's core feelings. If you judge yourself or others negatively for experiencing a "negative" emotion, this will probably create conflict. This conflict can exist intrapsychically, or within yourself, or interpersonally, or another person judging you.

It is important to note here that not all negative responses to negative emotions are bad. Sometimes there are good reasons to have a negative reaction or response to "bad" feelings. The primitive response of emotions creates action in an individual. For example, if you feel shame you want to submit, but anger will make you want to punish. Fear encourages you to run away. These responses are not always bad. But in the human and modern world, you need to act with more consciousness than impulse. Your response to an emotion needs to consider long-term implications and can be a complicated process. Think again of a parent responding to a child's emotional needs. If the parent responded from a raw and impulsive state, would their response benefit the child 20 years later in their life? If all people only followed raw and impulsive responses and reactions, there would be major trouble. This is where "good logic" is required to help you determine judgment on "overly emotional" responses.

But there is a cost to inhibiting and judging feelings. This is easily seen in people who suppress, avoid, distract, or repress feelings as they emerge. Not processing this state of being does not mean it just dissipates. It just lingers in the back of the mind, waiting to be dealt with. Think of it like "unfinished business." These emotions are there to tell you about important information related to your goals and/or needs. If it has not done its "job" yet to communicate this to you, it needs to hang around until it does.

This can be a problem when someone is avoiding negative emotions constantly. More and more "unfinished business" is crammed in the back of your mind, waiting to come out. In addition, the self-consciousness system will probably start amping up its negative response inner "dialogue." You may find yourself thinking, "This is stupid to feel like this, you are stupid," or "What is wrong with you for feeling this way?" When this happens, and this dialogue occurs consistently, the original feelings become stifled. And this dialogue begins to develop their own core feelings. For example, the part of you that is made of core feelings will be judged and wounded by your self-consciousness system. This is a tough and negative cycle to be stuck in. Basically, your consciousness has turned on itself. And this often then leads to depression.

Now, remember back to how people deal with their emotional system at the start of this chapter. People do not all respond the same way to negative situations. Some are more sensitive than others, which is "trait neuroticism." When someone has high trait neuroticism, they will most likely struggle with these challenges. This is because their negative feelings are stronger than other people's. This intense response can develop complex interpersonal relationships, primarily for those who do not have a good foundation or framework for understanding this information. Sadly, most do not.

Another important item to recognize is that suppressed emotions are not processed yet. This means they are "lurking" in the background, waiting to be released. This creates a vulnerability for that person, meaning that if something happens that triggers or releases this "unfinished business," it can lead to an unexpected and uncontrollable release. Think about people who "fly off the handle," or "erupt" emotionally. Or maybe someone has an anxiety attack or attempts suicide. These are individuals who have attempted to hold back their negative emotions. But after a while, the "back of the mind" gets full, a trigger happens, and all those things needing attention rush up and out. Combined with all the other things back there, this can turn into a very raw and uncontrolled situation. The emotions are powerful and primitive, often creating a situation where a person cannot stop their consciousness from acting on the impulses of those negative emotions. And a display of this painful and impulsive response tends to end up with even more problems than solutions. But instead of recognizing that this reaction was due to maladaptive emotional response systems, the person is often more determined than ever to try to suppress their negative emotions, compounding the issue and setting them up to repeat the same reaction again in the future.

So using this information you can begin to deduce how to process emotions in an adaptive manner. First, re-examine what a maladaptive process involves:

- Not fully comprehending what an emotion is
- Deny or avoid negative emotions, commonly paired with criticism of the self to enforce inhibition
- When the blocks or inhibition fails, an excessive and uncontrollable emotional display

No flip those steps to create an adaptive approach:

1. Provide effective education to create awareness of what an emotion is and how human consciousness functions
2. Encourage people and interpersonal relationships to be aware and attuned to emotions and how they respond to information about personal goals and needs
3. Allow healthy regulation of impulses connected with stronger emotions to support long-term goals and values

The goal of this approach is to find the "sweet spot." Allow someone to be aware of their own emotions, regulate their emotions when they are powerful and strong. Being aware and responsive or adaptive is a fine balance but possible when there is an environment, both interpersonal and intrapsychic, to support this goal.

For instance, the example of a parent responding to an emotional child. The one choice, to chastise the child, is wrought with problems because it does not create an environment for being aware of the emotion and supporting regulation. It is also punitive and inhibitory. This type of response can lead to the child internalizing his or her emotions, creating a problem with regulation and attunement. On the other hand, responding with just an "I am sorry you are upset, etc." is good, but is just the beginning. It helps the child identify their emotions, which is part of the best environment; however, what follows needs to then allow the child to learn how to regulate their intense emotions. This can be an identification that the situation is not life or death, and that it is normal to experience the situation (if indeed it is normal). For instance, if the child is upset because they stubbed their toe on the chair, you can express awareness of the feeling, pain, and that it is not dire, by explaining all people stub their toes and it will feel better soon. You can even offer the choice to continue playing in that area or that game, or an alternative that would minimize the physical requirements or that specific location. This response follows this process:

1. State that you are aware of the emotion and what the feeling expressed was intended to communicate
2. Offer comments that identify the severity or lack of severity of the situation with a positive focus. The comments also lack an element of shame, and also offer solutions to the situation related to the experience

Not long ago, when the world was hard and living life was harder, the mentality of "suck it up," was reigning. Every person struggled and hustled to survive, so each person was required to deal with their "problems" on their own. This was the environment those that lived during the Great Depression and World War II lived in. But over the last three decades, the quality of life has shifted dramatically. Now, many people are sensitive to the negative emotions that all humans deal with. In addition, there are places where negative emotions are identified as "just" in their full expression. This comes with its own set of issues. For example, think about coaching or teaching children. Many approaches remove the responsibility of a child's negative emotion onto the coach or teacher, not the child, because no criticism is allowed. It is focused solely on "positive reinforcement." No negative feedback is allowed because it might hurt the child's feelings. Not only does this deprive a child the opportunity to learn about attunement and regulation of their emotions, but it also sends the message that any "criticism," even constructive criticism from a supportive source, is harmful and bad.
Another example of this swing of the pendulum in response to negative emotions is censoring speech for fear of "offending" someone. At times, yes, this is necessary. For example, censoring language for children or choosing

words that do not negatively stereotype others, but in other situations, this is a problem. It makes the communicator responsible for another person's negative emotion, rather than teach people how to recognize and adapt their responses to these situations. Think about it like this, you are giving a presentation about a product you are selling. You mention that you are "targeting" a particular audience. During your presentation, someone raises their hand and comments, "Please do not use the word targeting. The customers who shop here would find that offensive and some have trauma that would be triggered because of this word." This person is now expecting you to shoulder the potential negative emotional response of others, not even in the room, because of an innocuous word chosen for the presentation (which is also a fairly common word used in business and marketing methods).

While people are becoming more sensitive, and even aware of their emotions, both "good" and "bad" feelings, there is a lack of education surrounding emotional response and a lack of communication regarding awareness, attunement, and adaptive regulation of all emotions, including the stronger negative ones. Educating humans about human consciousness, the conflicts, and surrounding feelings, is important for the future. If you can view your emotions as a message and information being shared with your brain about an experience, and not a problem that you should avoid, you can begin to solve problems and work through challenging situations much easier. The best way to do this is by:

- Encourage curiosity and accepting attitude towards emotions and responses;
- Allow awareness and attunement of personal feelings, as well as the feelings of others;
- Recognize that the information these emotions are sharing is related to goals and needs, and determining what it is connected with;
- Identify the primal nature of emotions that are often short-sighted and impulsive, which are not always necessary or relevant in this complicated and fast-paced world today; and
- Learn adaptive techniques for problematic emotions to regulate specific aspects of that emotion so it can still align with your long-term goals and values.

Emotions and the Vagus Nerve

Your blood pressure lowers and heart rate slows down when the Vagus nerve is stimulated. This is scientifically shown in most healthy and fully-functioning humans. Also, it is scientifically shown time and time again that slow, deep, long breaths also help lower your blood pressure and your heart rate to slow down. Your heart is an important organ that has influence over many of the other organs in your body. When it is stressed, other organs become stressed. And the same is true on the opposite side; when your heart is calm and relaxed, the other organs in your body can become calm and relaxed. It even helps calm your cells down, it is that powerful. When your cells and organs are relaxed, your body can send and receive messages better with your brain. This, in turn, allows you to handle the emotional pendulum more efficiently.

Otto Loewi, a physiologist from Germany, identified the connection between a stimulated Vagus nerve and acetylcholine, a neurotransmitter. It was early in the 1920's when Loewi recognized that the Vagus nerve sent the message to release this, and its primary function is to calm the body and mind when it is experiencing stress. And one of the best and easiest methods for triggering the release of this neurotransmitter is by breathing deeply very slowly. You have probably heard of people recommending taking a "deep breath" when things are stressful or they appear emotionally agitated. Or maybe you have even tried calming yourself down with deep breaths as you count to ten. What you may not have realized is that this advice is really guiding you to self-stimulate your Vagus nerve in order to release acetylcholine, ultimately resulting in a calmer body and mind.

"Controlling" your Vagus nerve, or learning how to work with it, is important because you can keep it functioning properly. If it becomes over-stimulated, you can experience responses like emotional disturbances, added stress, and anxiety. Another powerful tool that can be combined with deep breathing practices to stimulate your Vagus nerve is visualization. This combination results in amazing, peaceful bodies and minds. Visualization is also a scientifically proven method for helping calm emotions and responses. You may have heard famous business people, athletes, and leaders talking about their visualization process. They use it because it works! As you stimulate your Vagus nerve with your deep breathing skills, you can support yourself as you work through challenging and strong emotional situations.

Chapter 3: Common Symptoms of a Malfunctioning Vagus Nerve

Some may say that the Vagus nerve is the most important cranial nerve in your body. Others may disagree that it is the most important, but almost everyone can agree that it is vital to your well-being. Your optimal health, your most healthy life, requires a properly functioning Vagus nerve. The nerve does extend through some of your most vital organs and systems, such as your brain, esophagus, heart, lungs, and digestive tract. It also has the widest distribution of sensory and motor nerves in the body. It is responsible for the things in your body that you do not need to think about, like digestion and heart rate. It is pretty important.

But what happens when things go wrong? That is when you get disorders and malfunctions. Your Vagus nerve can be underactive or overactive. An overactive Vagus nerve can lead to increased stress and anxiety. An underactive Vagus nerve can lead to gastroparesis, which then can lead to diabetes. Before things get too "bad," you will typically get some warning signs. These symptoms are messages that there is either a disorder or damage to your Vagus nerve. Chances are, if you notice these symptoms, especially early on, you can do something about it. And most likely the best thing for you to do is to stimulate your Vagus nerve.

As mentioned above, your Vagus nerve can be overstimulated or under-stimulated. This means your symptoms can be classified under one "type" of problem or another. Sometimes the symptoms will overlap, but for the most part, you can identify the underlying issue for your Vagus nerve and take steps to correct it. One of the most common issues with Vagus nerve malfunctions is that it appears to be IBS or Irritable Bowel Syndrome. The symptoms can be similar. In addition, physicians have a hard time diagnosing the condition in the Vagus nerve, primarily because the conditions do not usually show up in routine testing unless things have become really bad.

Vagus Nerve Damage – Common Symptoms

Before going any further regarding the malfunction, it is important to recognize the most common symptoms:

- Pain
- Organ Dysfunction

- Muscle Cramps
- Difficulty Swallowing
- Fainting
- Peptic Ulcer
- Gastroparesis

Pain and the Vagus Nerve

The common symptom for a malfunctioning Vagus nerve is a pain. But to know that the pain you are feeling is related to your Vagus nerve requires you to identify how the pain manifested in your body, where it is happening, and what the pain is trying to tell you. You need to understand the pain you are experiencing. Vagus nerve pain is caused by pressure, trauma, or injury that is mechanical. This leads to inflammation and swelling. Most of the time the pain you are experiencing is from a pinched nerve. The nerve leaves the skull through small foramina. This pain is vague and relatively flat. It is not constant nor sharp. It will not feel like someone is stabbing you or lasting for stretches of time.

Organ Dysfunction and the Vagus Nerve

This nerve is long. Like mentioned earlier, it goes through several different important organs. When there is damage to the nerve, the organs fail to get the signal from the brain and the brain fails to get the information it needs from the organs. If there is damage to the nerve fibers the symptoms you will feel will be localized and represent symptoms of organ dysfunction. This does not result in your organs not working all of a sudden but it does mean that some of the function will be less or absent.

Muscle Cramps and the Vagus Nerve

The Vagus nerve has the primary function of offering stimulation to the vocal chord's muscles. If you Vagus nerve has any sort of damage or dysfunction, there is a probability that these muscles will be damaged as well. This then interferes with both your breathing ability and your voice. There are other muscles that are supported by the function of the Vagus nerve as well. You may feel like your electrolytes are low, such as your potassium or magnesium levels, which cause muscle cramps, but those cramps may also be caused by damage to your Vagus nerve.

Difficulty Swallowing and the Vagus Nerve

As mentioned earlier, the Vagus nerve is responsible for your esophagus and vocal chord function; however, when there is a problem with the Vagus nerve, there can be a problem. One of those problems includes your gag reflex. Just like a patient who has suffered from a stroke or head trauma and has trouble swallowing now, when a patient has damage to their Vagus nerve, they can experience trouble swallowing. If you are having trouble swallowing and also have a change to your gag reflex it is likely that you have a problem with your Vagus nerve. The major worry with this is the increased risk of choking. The start is just general challenges with swallowing and compounds from there.

Fainting and the Vagus Nerve

Fainting is a serious side effect of the Vagus nerve malfunction. This is a symptom of an overstimulated and overactive Vagus nerve. When you get this sudden fainting symptom you can collapse. The action of fainting is not necessarily dangerous by itself, but then, you collapse because of it, you increase the risk of physical injury.

Peptic ulcer and the Vagus Nerve

If there is damage to the Vagus nerve, another symptom and condition of this damage can be the development of a peptic ulcer. The damage of the nerve may be stopping the beneficial mechanisms of control, which are in charge of the secretion of gastric acid. When this impairment occurs you may end secreting more peptic acid than normal. This then results in various conditions and diseases related to the gastrointestinal tract, like ulceration, gastroesophageal reflux disease, and dyspepsia.

Gastroparesis and the Vagus Nerve

This condition has been mentioned a couple of times already and now deserves its own listing of symptoms for a dysfunction of the Vagus nerve. This is caused when your Vagus nerve is underactive. When this happens there is a negative impact on the blood supply to your stomach after you ingest food. When this happens, it is common to feel painful cramping or a stabbing sensation in your abdomen. You may also experience painful spasms. This painful reaction can then lead to heartburn, nausea, and unintended weight loss. It will also likely impact your typical intake of food.

More on Gastroparesis

This is a serious condition that impacts the typical and spontaneous stomach muscle movement. In more healthy humans, the contractions in your stomach are strong propulsion for your food to move into your digestive tract. But if you suffer from gastroparesis, the movement in your stomach muscles is slower or not functioning at all. This stops your stomach from emptying the contents like it is supposed to.

Similar symptoms to this can be caused by things like high blood pressure, various antidepressants, and opioid pain relievers. And if you suffer from gastroparesis, these can exacerbate the condition.

Vomiting and nausea can be caused by interference with common digestion. It can also interfere with nutrient levels and blood sugar. Unfortunately, the cause of this malfunction is unknown in most cases. It can be a result of diabetes complications or after surgery. The unfortunate reality is that there is no cure to this illness but there are things you can do to offer some relief to the symptoms.

If you suspect you have gastroparesis, see if you can mark one or more of the symptoms below:

- Malnutrition
- Unintentional weight loss
- Loss of appetite
- Alterations to blood sugar levels
- Pain in the abdomen
- Bloating in the stomach
- Acid reflux
- After a few hours, food is still undigested, which is most evident in vomit
- Vomiting
- Feeling full after a few bites
- Nausea

But you may also have gastroparesis with no symptoms or signs that you easily notice. If you have some symptoms or signs that worry you and you are concerned you are suffering from this illness, you should make an appointment to discuss your concerns with your doctor.

Again, it is not always readily evident what causes this condition, but when it is clear what causes it, it is most often related to the damage or dysfunction of the Vagus nerve. The Vagus nerve is vital to the control of your stomach muscles, so when it is not working right, this can be the cause. It also influences your digestion. This means if there is a problem with it, chances are that your stomach has lost or minimized its ability to move the food from your stomach into the small intestine. This leaves food in your stomach instead of moving it into digestion and gathering the nutrients from it.

Your Vagus nerve can be damaged from a variety of sources, such as surgery or diabetes. It is particularly common to experience this illness when you have surgery on your small intestine or stomach. Other factors that can increase your risk of developing gastroparesis include:

- Hypothyroidism or an underactive thyroid
- Multiple sclerosis, Parkinson's disease or other nervous system diseases
- Scleroderma, which is a disease in of your connective tissue.
- Narcotic pain medications, or other medicines that can reduce the speed of food emptying from the stomach into the intestines.
- Infections, typically a viral infection
- Surgery of your esophagus or abdomen
- Diabetes

Men are less likely to develop gastroparesis than women.

There are many complications to this disease. Some of these complications include:

- Reduced quality of life.
- Unexpected and unanticipated blood sugar fluctuations
- Leftover food in your stomach that is undigested and hardens
- Malnutrition
- Severe dehydration

Daily and life responsibilities can become a challenge when there is a flare-up of symptoms. It can be very uncomfortable and painful to do everyday activities like work and family actions. Also, while gastroparesis does not lead directly to diabetes, the constant changes the amount and the volume of food passing into the small intestine can cause major fluctuations to your blood sugar levels. If you suffer from diabetes, this can make that disease worse. In addition, not being able to control your blood sugar levels, in turn, makes the gastroparesis condition worse, too.

When food stays in your stomach and does not get digested, it can turn into a hard mass in your stomach. This hardened mass is called a "bezoar." This can lead to vomiting and nausea. It can all be a life-threatening situation because it can stop all food from getting into your small intestine. This can lead to starvation at the extreme but malnutrition as well. This is because your body is not digesting the nutrients you are consuming but also because of the pain you are probably experiencing in your stomach, you are most likely not eating as much. This limits the amount of calories you are consuming. Also, you can suffer from malnutrition because of vomiting. You do not have enough time to absorb the nutrients you consume if you vomit right away. Also, vomiting leads to severe dehydration.

There are several tests you can undergo, under the supervision and treatment of a doctor. The purpose of these tests is to rule out other potential illnesses with similar symptoms. Some of the common tests used to diagnose gastroparesis include:

- Gastric emptying study
- Upper gastrointestinal endoscopy
- Ultrasound
- Upper gastrointestinal series

The process of the gastric emptying study includes some of the most important information in making a gastroparesis diagnosis. Your medical professional will instruct you to eat a small meal, like an egg or two with a piece of toast, along with a little bit of radioactive material. Then a scanner is used to watch the movement of this radioactive material in your body. It is placed on your abdomen to watch the rate of food removal from your stomach. If you are taking medication that can slow down stomach emptying, you will need to stop them for the study. If you are unsure if your medication interferes with this you should ask your medical professional about it.

The upper GI, or gastrointestinal, endoscopy requires the use of a camera on a long tube to examine the digestive tract. It goes through your esophagus, stomach, and the upper part of your small intestine, also called the duodenum. This test is also used to diagnose other conditions like pyloric stenosis and peptic ulcer disease. The symptoms of these diseases can be similar to the symptoms of gastroparesis.

Ultrasounds are great tests for producing images of your internal body without entering it with radioactive materials or cameras on tubing. It uses sound waves that operate at a high frequency to create the images. This test is used to help diagnose problems with your kidneys or gallbladder, which could also be causing your symptoms. Another test that occurs on the exterior of your body are x-rays of your digestive tract; however, most often for testing for gastroparesis, your medical professional will require you to drink a liquid that is chalky and white, called barium, which coats your digestive tract to highlight any abnormalities in the x-ray.

The best way to treat this dysfunction is to recognize the condition causing it and treat that. For example, if diabetes is causing it, you need to treat and control your diabetes. If it is caused by damage to your Vagus nerve, you should treat and stimulate your nerve.

Some of the common treatment options include:

- Change to your diet
- Medications
- Surgery

Diet and Gastroparesis

Making sure you get appropriate nutrients is important to your overall health. One of the most important goals of treating gastroparesis is to make sure you get the nutrition necessary for a well-balanced life. Most people can control and manage their gastroparesis with a healthy diet. For this reason, your medical professional may instruct you to work with a dietician to find foods and drinks that are easily digestible so you can make sure you get enough nutrients and calories from what you consume. Some of the following suggestions are common advice from a dietician regarding gastroparesis:

- Stay away from vegetables and fruits that are high in fiber, like broccoli and oranges, which are common bezoar instigators.
- Avoid raw vegetables and fruits, opting for well-cooked versions instead.
- Make sure to chew your food thoroughly.
- Eat frequent, small meals.
- Favor foods that are low-fat with small servings of food high in good fat if you can tolerate them.

- Select pureed foods and soups often because they are easier to swallow.
- Drink a large amount of water every day, between 34 and 51 ounces each day.
- After eating a snack or meal, do gentle exercises, like going for a walk or casual bike ride.
- Stay away from known triggers and unhealthy behaviors, like drinking alcohol, smoking, or drinking carbonated beverages.
- After eating a snack or meal, try not to lie down for at least two hours after.
- Take a multivitamin every day.

Some recommended foods include:

- Yogurt (without fruit pieces)
- White crackers
- White bread and rolls and "light" whole-wheat bread without nuts or seeds
- Vegetable juice
- Vegetable broth
- Tuna (packed in water)
- Tomato sauce, paste, puree, juice
- Tofu
- Strained meat baby food
- Rice
- Puffed wheat and rice cereals
- Potatoes, white or sweet (no skin)
- Plain or egg bagels
- Peaches and pears (canned)
- Pasta
- Pancakes
- Mushrooms (cooked)
- Milk, if tolerated
- Lean beef, veal and pork (not fried)
- Fruit juices and drinks
- Frozen yogurt
- Flour or corn tortillas
- English muffins

- Eggs
- Custard and pudding
- Cream of wheat or rice
- Crab, lobster, shrimp, clams, scallops, oysters
- Cottage cheese
- Chicken or turkey (no skin and not fried)
- Carrots (cooked)
- Beets (cooked)
- Bananas
- Baked french fries
- Baby food vegetables and fruits
- Applesauce

There are a variety of medications you can take to also treat gastroparesis. These medications can include medicines to help trigger your stomach muscles and to control vomiting and nausea. One medication, metoclopramide has very serious side effects, but erythromycin can stop being as effective with continued use and lead to side effects like diarrhea. Domperidone is a new medication that has fewer side effects than the other two but it is restricted until more information is available. These three medicines are prescribed to stimulate your stomach muscles. The medications used to prevent nausea include Zofran, Benadryl, Unisom, and Compro.

If the condition is severe enough, surgery may be considered. This is typically only done when a person cannot tolerate any liquids or foods. This is a serious situation in which a medical professional will most likely place the feeding tube into the small intestine or insert a gastric venting tube to help relieve the pressure caused by the gastric contents.

A feeding tube can be inserted through your mouth or nose into your small intestine, or they can be passed through your skin into it. The tube is often a temporary situation and only utilized when the condition is severe or when the person's blood sugar cannot be controlled any other way. In some cases, a parenteral or IV feeding tube is needed and it is inserted into a vein in his or her chest.

There are medications and treatments under investigation. One such new medication being explored is relamorelin. In trials, this medication helped speed up the emptying of the gastric system. It can also help reduce vomiting. It is not approved by the FDA currently. There are larger trials being conducted. Therapies being explored include the aide of endoscopy. One such therapy involved using endoscopy to insert a tube or stent into the location where the small intestine connects to the stomach. This is intended to keep that space open at all times so food can pass through easily. There are several studies using "botox," or botulinum toxin, using endoscopy but none have had success. It is currently not a recommended treatment. Finally, there is another option being explored currently, a surgery that is considered minimally invasive in order to place the feeding tube into the small intestine directly.

There are things that you can do at home to help treat this condition as well. These include stopping smoking, losing weight if overweight, and learning deep breathing techniques. Other "alternative" or at-home treatments people can use, although more studies are needed for most of these, include:

- Acupuncture
- Electroacupuncture
- STW 5 or iberogast, an herbal combination developed in Germany
- Rikkunshito, an herbal combination developed in Japan
- Cannabis

Ways to Treat a Malfunction of the Vagus Nerve

If you experience one or more of the symptoms above, you should begin immediately treating the dysfunction. The benefit of treating the malfunction is that it also results in support of a healthy Vagus nerve, preventing new damage to the nerve in the future. As mentioned in the previous chapter, Vagus nerve stimulation is one form of treatment, although it is often only used in a clinical setting for certain illnesses. There are things you can do yourself to help stimulate the nerve; however, which include deep breathing techniques.

When you stimulate your Vagus nerve, you can improve conditions like Alzheimer's disease, poor blood circulation, leaky gut, unstable moods, chronic heart failure, memory problems, bulimia, obesity, migraines, OCD, heart disease, and anxiety.

Other techniques to self-stimulate the Vagus nerve include:

- Engaging your abdominal muscles
- Acupuncture

- Chewing gum
- Prayer
- Resting on your right side
- Tai chi
- Massage
- Fasting, particularly intermittent fasting
- Laughter
- Engaging in positive social relationships and situations
- Yoga
- Meditation
- Chanting
- Singing
- Cold showers

If you suffer from severe gastroparesis, some medical professionals may recommend the use of a feeding tube to help make sure you get the correct nutrients directly into your intestines, preventing malnutrition. You could also be prescribed other various medication to help the dysfunction. If you suffer from a symptom, such as fainting, it is likely a medical professional will prescribe medication to help manage those situations. Two common fainting-prevention medications include paroxetine and sertraline.

Chapter 4: An Introduction to the Polyvagal Theory

Developmental outcomes, physiology, and social engagement are explored in the neurobiological theory, the polyvagal theory. It is a complicated theory that can get convoluted. The design of this chapter is to help break down the theory into a three-part introduction. To begin, you need to know more about stress and the physiology of it as well as various responses to stress that occur in your body.

Your Nervous System

There are two primary nervous systems in your body, your peripheral nervous system, or PNS, and your central nervous system, or CNS. The CNS is your spinal cord and brain. It controls thoughts. The PNS is all the other nerves as well as ganglia. These regulate the limbs, organs, and muscles. In the PNS is the autonomic nervous system, or ANS, and the somatic nervous system. Both are responsible for involuntary and voluntary functioning. For example, talking, seeing, smelling, as well as digesting and breathing. Then the ANS is broken down to the parasympathetic and sympathetic nervous system. This is the "fight, flight, or freeze" impulse and "rest and digest." When you relax and let yourself be calm, you signal your parasympathetic nervous system to "rest and digest." But if you become afraid or stressed, you have a physiological response. This is your sympathetic nervous system, or your "fight, flight, or freeze" response. Your body is responding to mobilize and handle the "threat." Your heart beats faster, pupils dilate, saliva production increases, and your blood sugar increases.

When you are threatened or afraid, the model is fairly straightforward. Your body responds to a problem. But there are a lot of things that are still unanswered or are a variable. For instance, is there always either a parasympathetic response or a sympathetic response or can you operate without one of those responses? How does the body respond when the body is chronically stressed? Why does a body trigger the "fight, flight, or freeze" response when you see something dramatic on television when you know it is not real or is not life-threatening. Are emotions necessary for these responses?

Humans are "hard-wired" to be social and in groups. This means that social engagement is entangled with how you respond physiologically. This has led to humans coping with stressors that are urgent and impactful on the immediate self but also stressors that are social in nature, too. This theory, the polyvagal theory, attempts to stitch together factors of these such responses on a social, physiological, and evolutionary platform. But before getting into these factors, it is good to have a review of the Vagus nerve and how it deals with the regulation of your stress levels.

The Vagus Nerve and Stress Regulation

This "wandering" nerve that stretches from your brainstem to your colon has about 80% of its nerve fibers working in one capacity; to send information from the organs in your body to your brain. This type of nerve fiber is called afferent fibers. This information alerts your brain about what your organs are doing, like if your heart is beating at a normal rate or faster, or if you are having trouble with digestion or if it is functioning properly, or if your pupils are dilated or not. The other almost 20% of the nerves are efferent, or "highways" for the brain to tell your organs to do different things. This will be discussed in more detail later in this chapter. The Vagus nerve has a very important role in the regulation of the body. Its primary job is to make sure everything is balanced with one another. This is called "homeostasis." This relates to things like body temperature, chemistry in your body, activation, etc. And what is even more amazing is that the homeostasis of an organ can be different depending on the context of the situation, meaning the Vagus nerve interprets the context in which you are living and works with the organs to respond evenly to that.

To help illustrate this point, think about what happens to your body when the weather is hot. Blood takes a longer route, moving around your body to spread out the heat, but when the temperatures drop and it is cold outside, your blood changes its average course, favoring your major organs over your extremities. Even the arteries in your legs and arms constrict in the cold to minimize the amount of blood flowing into them so it can keep your organs warm. It may be frustrating to suffer from cold fingers and toes but it is your body's way of keeping your body temperature balanced for your internal organs. Next time you experience this, take a moment to thank your Vagus nerve for doing its job and put on warmer clothing without complaint!

Social stressors can also change the equilibrium of your body. The average heart beats between 60 and 80 times every minute when it is relaxed. But if a bear chases you, or you are running a marathon, your heart should pump faster to spread more oxygen out. In both scenarios, the primary goal for your body is to go a further distance. The extra blood and oxygen are being utilized to help you reach that goal. But when you feel nervous or see something disturbing on television your heart also picks up the pace. Think about before the first day of work, the morning of a big exam, preparing to walk on stage for a large presentation, etc. All of these situations typically lead to a faster heart rate. These situations may seem strange to have more blood and oxygen racing around your body. You are not preparing your body to fight or run, but your body is responding like it is. It is acting the same as if a bear all of a sudden rounded the corner to maul you, instead of just saying hello to a nice, attractive, special person. These "other" situations are explained in the polyvagal theory to define why this happens.

"Polyvagal" is used to describe the branches of the Vagus nerve. There are two types; unmyelinated and myelinated. A Myelin Sheath is a substance primarily made of fat that lines various nerves. It is meant to aid signals so they are sent to the brain faster and more accurately. If a nerve does not have a myelin sheath, it is called unmyelinated and it functions more primitively. The messaging from these nerves is not as fast or organized. To help you visualize the difference between the two, think about cars traveling on a well-designed and maintained road with strategic stoplights and a speed limit sign. The road is designed to help passengers travel quickly and easily but is controlled to maintain the safety of all the passengers on it. This is a "myelinated" road. Now visualize a dirt road winding around backcountry with no regulations in place and no clear direction. The journey is more troublesome and dangerous for all the travels passing along it. In addition, with the bumps and the uneven surface, it is harder to travel quickly. This is an "unmyelinated" road.

The branches of the Vagus nerve, and all the nerves in the body, are meant to keep your body balanced and functioning well. This is accomplished with three neural control stages. These three stages are operating in the unmyelinated branch of the Vagus nerve, the sympathetic adrenal system, and the myelinated branch of the Vagus nerve. There are different times for operation and a variety of effects each stage produces in and on the body when it is activated.

The unmyelinated branch of the Vagus nerve can be considered the least evolved of all the stages. This is because it is a more primitive evolution of communication in the body, and it is seen in primitive vertebrates, amphibians, and various reptiles as well. As animals evolved, coping skills for stress evolved to be more effective on a physiological level.

Below is a table that outlines the different stages, from least evolved to the most, along with the behavioral functions each stage deals with.

Stage Number	Component Utilized	Behavior and Function	"Lower Motor Neurons"
3	Myelinated branch of the Vagus nerve	Inhibits sympathetic-adrenal influences, related to calming and social-soothing as well as social communication	Nucleus ambiguus
2	Sympathetic-adrenal System	Actively avoiding, mobilization	Spinal cord
1	Unmyelinated branch of the Vagus nerve	Passive avoidance, feigning death, immobilized	Dorsal motor nucleus of the Vagus nerve

There is a fine balance struck between inhibition and excitation. This means that when one is active, the others are inactive. When one is "on," the others are "off." When you are facing common, everyday stress, like a deadline at work of having a fight with your partner or having a lot of homework to do, your body tends to suppress two states, favoring the reliance on your more evolved step, the myelinated Vagus nerve. But when stress becomes too great, your body drops to the next stage, which is more primitive. And then further, if compounded.

Unmyelinated Vagus Nerve Introduction

This is the most primitive response to your environment. This is about immobilization or even fainting, which is common in humans at this stage. Animals feign death when activating their unmyelinated Vagus nerve. The main goal of this response is to conserve your resources. This is especially seen in your heart rate. Bradycardia, or a low, maintained heart rate, is often the outcome of this state. Some animals and most reptiles use this to mimic death, but humans need more oxygen than these animals. In fact, all mammals would suffer severe damage if they feigned death in this manner. To see examples of this, research sharks when they go into the "shark trance" or snakes when they experience tonic immobility. It is clear that this response is not always very effective, which is most likely why humans have evolved to not use this response often. You probably will not be in this stage on a regular basis, certainly not during your day-to-day activities. This stage is activated only when there is extreme stress.

If someone experiences this stress and response chronically, they suffer from an illness called "vasovagal syncope." These people faint when they are triggered in different situations or experience extreme stress. Emotional triggers are also known to cause this response for people with this diagnosis, such as seeing blood. It can also occur from standing too long. It is unknown what causes this disorder but some experiments conducted on animals suggest it is the sudden activation of the unmyelinated Vagus nerve that creates this result. In addition, this disorder can be a life-long struggle or it can appear only when a person is under extreme stress.

Sympathetic – Adrenal System

This second stage in the profess mobilizes the "fight, flight or freeze" response. When your body detects a threat, it can respond in this primitive fashion. This response uses up a lot of energy and therefore typically only engage it when there is a threat to your environment that makes you feel unsafe. The activation of this response is often subconscious because we are constantly observing and analyzing the environment. This is called neuroception. You may not know it, but you are constantly evaluating the places and situations you are in to determine if you are safe or threatened.

There is a difference between neuroception, perception, and sensation. The sensation is how your body receives an input from the senses and is a completely physiological response. Perception, on the other hand, is how you process the various sensations you experience. People can sense the same things, like look at the same picture, but they perceive it differently. Neuroception does not align with either of these experiences. It is all about how you decide if something is safe or not for you. For instance, you may not think the disagreement you are having with someone is unsafe or threatening, but your mind interprets clues like facial expressions, tone of voice, appearance, and decide it is a threat to you. This is a subconscious interpretation of stimuli and cues appearing in that context. You are not just perceiving the stimuli but also deciding if the environment you are in is safe or not because of that stimuli. This is a great response to have evolved because it allows animals and humans to leave once a predator is perceived.

This is a response best for physical danger, but sometimes it is activated in psychologically stressing situations, as well. For instance, you want to speak to a special person you want to make a good impression on. During an encounter with this person, something happens where you become embarrassed. On the outside, you may appear calm, or you may try to tell yourself to calm down, but often your face will reveal what is happening. Your face may turn red and become hot. Your heartbeat increases. Palms become sweaty. These responses are part of the sympathetic-adrenal system. There is an emotional threat present that your body perceived and it is responding as if that were a physical threat to your life. For animals, this is very helpful. But for humans in day-to-day societal and social engagement, it is not the most adaptive response stage.

The third stage in the process is the most complex. It is integrated and evolved to allow you to interact with your environment in a high-functioning manner. This is called the "social engagement system." This system regulates face and head striated muscles and the visceral organs regulated by the myelinated Vagus nerve. It is a two-part process; it first regulates the psychological "distance" from threats, and then by straining engagement and stimuli from other situations. As an example, when infants recognize the face of their mothers, they feel a sense of security. The process reduces the "distance" between the infant and the mother by listening to her voice and using their vocal abilities to communicate with her. To increase the engagement the infant may then make sure to keep their eyes open and trained on their mother, as well as shift their body to face her more. This system is responsible for controlling facial muscles, meaning it is valuable in communicating emotions and showing listening skills and visual recognition. All the individual functions involved use a large number of cranial nerves thanks to the neural circuit system. All of this starts in the cortex.

When you feel threatened, your stage 2, "fight, flight, or freeze," sympathetic-adrenal system is triggered. When you are secure and safe, your stage 3, "social engagement system," myelinated Vagus nerve is triggered.

This stage 3 inhibits the response to stress and activates the nerves in the cranium to encourage engagement. In this process, the Vagus nerve is just one of the cranial nerves stimulated.

Throughout this process, it is important to recognize that animals primarily only had an unmyelinated Vagus nerve to activate the parasympathetic action. Over time mammals evolved to have the myelinated Vagus nerve as well to align social engagement with parasympathetic action. In the medulla, the various cranial nerves converge with the Vagus nerve. Here, they can instigate responses that are similar and coordinated. For instance, when there is a feeling of security, the medulla in the brainstem signals various cranial nerves to align activity and social engagement. This requires the Vagus nerve to be an active participant in the social engagement system in your body.

The Vagal Tone

There are a lot of cranial nerves engaging in the system, with many parallel functions as the Vagus nerve, so it stands to reason there may be some confusion about what the Vagus nerve is doing in the social engagement system specifically. The internal organs of your body are connected to the brain by the connection created by the activated myelinated Vagus nerve, which is activated with the use of the social engagement system. Many of the other cranial nerves are associated with the face and neck. The Vagus nerve, on the other hand, is connected to the internal organs, which many people would not necessarily consider part of the social engagement system. But your internal organs and their impacted body parts need to know if there is a threat or not, so they can respond appropriately. For instance, in a secure state, your body relaxes its internal systems, allowing digestion to operate at a stable level, the heart to beat at a relaxed rate, the breath can slow, etc. But when there is a threat, it all changes. This activity created in your body is called the "vagal tone." This primarily deals with the amount of blood moving from the Vagus nerve to the various organs in your body it impacts. An engaged system allows the Vagus nerve to "talk" to the parts of the body through the passage of blood, meaning there is a high vagal tone.

The easiest place to observe this process is in the heart. The sinoatrial node is made of cells that are a natural regulator for your heart rate. The cells in this node are responsible for your rhythmic heart rate. Left unchecked, the rate of this heartbeat is much faster than your body needs while at rest. Left alone, the pace is about 110 beats per minute, while a resting heart rate for a healthy adult is between 60 and 80 beats per minute. To help stabilize this and relax the body through the heart rate the vagal tone is inhibiting this "pacemaker." It is called the "vagal brake" in this situation because it is responsible for slowing the heart rate down. It is like driving a car. You can "floor" the gas pedal but the car will only move forward if you release the brake. One of the "side effects" of this vagal brake is that when you slow the heart rate down you end up inhaling at a faster rate than you exhale. Take a moment to observe your breath now. Do you inhale quickly and then have a longer time to allow the oxygen to circulate in your body before it is fully released? Chances are you have a longer exhale. This makes your resting heart "rhythm" more of a variable and labeled as "arrhythmic." There is a correlation between the variability of your heart rate and your vagal tone. This means that you can observe the variability in your heart rate as a measure of your vagal tone as well.

This how the body responds when it is resting and there is no perceived threat. But what happens when it senses something? When this "threat" is detected, the sympathetic system is activated, inhibiting the social engagement system. This means your myelinated Vagus nerve is much less active and there is a drop in the vagal tone amount. This means less inhibition on the heart rate, allowing it to beat faster with a stronger rhythm. This then moves your blood around your body faster, moving oxygen and sugar at a faster clip. When your vagal tone drops like this it is called "vagal suppression." It is like lifting your foot up from the brake so the car can go.

There is a hierarchy to the neural control stages outlined. The most often used stage is the use of the myelinated Vagus nerve because it encourages a relaxed body with little energy use. This allows your behavior to more social and uses less of your internal "resources" to function. This, in turn, promotes growth and overall health. But when there is a threat or perceived threat, your internal "resources" are used to support your "fight, flight, or freeze" response instead of promoting cortical processing. This is why you may find it hard to remember things from a stressful moment or why you're thinking is muddled in extremely stressful situations. This is the activation of the sympathetic-adrenal system. And if the situation is extreme enough, the third stage, immobilization, can be activated.

It is important to recognize there is a difference between the three stages and what happens when they are activated. When you recognize why your body is responding a certain way it is easier to handle stressors and avoid negative health issues, like developing chronic stress. Moving from one stage to another is a normal process and something you probably do a few times a week or month. It is an evolutionary process that is designed to help you survive and even thrive. Left unchecked; however, it can lead to poor health conditions. You do not want to be switching again and again in a day. Responding to stress daily or multiple times a day is hard on your body. Now with this understanding and introduction to the polyvagal theory, you have the tools to recognize various illnesses and create coping methods to support your body and Vagus nerve.

Chapter 5: Self-guided Healing Exercises to Balance the Vagus Nerve for Better Sleep, Injury Recovery, and Deep Relaxation

When your Vagus nerve is healthy it supports all sorts of parts of your body, including helping you sleep better, deeply relax, and even bounce back from injury faster. But how do you make sure this nerve stays healthy and properly functioning? Thankfully you can learn how to regulate this nerve on your own without the intervention of a medical professional, in most cases. When you know how to regulate and heal your Vagus nerve you can help reduce chronic inflammation, help you overcome migraines, reduce symptoms of chronic auto-immune disease, depression, and anxiety.

There is a scenario where you may no longer be able to accurately sense when something or someone is safe or not. This happens when you are chronically exposed to trauma for a long time. This means you could be in a safe situation but respond as if being threatened. You react by fighting, freezing, running away, or fainting. But over time and practice, you can learn how to "override" these responses to support a healthy response to a non-threatening situation. If you have a disorder affecting or originating from your Vagus nerve you can learn ways to stimulate your social engagement system. The more you practice this, the stronger the myelinated Vagus nerve pathway becomes. The more you activate this, the more fatty coating in the myelinated Vagal nerve, helping increase both control and speed of information sharing.

You can safely mobilize and immobilize your Vagus nerve using mind and body therapies that you can do at home. These therapies allow you to regulate the Vagus nerve and enhance your resilience. To be able to create this capacity, you first need to create the ability to feel connected, calm, and at peace. Being able to do this is the foundation. Then you can build upon it by tapping into your social engagement system and construct your tolerance for activation during distressing physiological situations. To achieve this you need to learn how to combine your social engagement system with both immobilization and mobilization, leading to a re-establishment of the sense of security while operating in those states of your nervous system.

Somatic psychology and the therapies for your mind and body require you to observe and engage in different present-moment situations, such as your thoughts, emotional experiences, breath, and the sensations in the body. These methodologies also assist you in observing and acknowledging your external environment, reaffirming that you are indeed safe in the present moment. Using physical movement is one form of these therapies, like walking meditations, tai chi, and yoga. Other therapies use complete stillness to help with this process. These include things like yoga Nidra, relaxation techniques, and supine or seated meditation.

An Example Practice for Healing Your Vagus Nerve

You can practice different engagement and stimulation of your Vagus nerve, using methods that require stillness and then others that require movement, so you practice blending social engagement for different energy and health requirements. The following example is designed to help your health and support your Vagus nerve.

1. Select a safe location. Identify and locate yourself in a non-threatening environment to begin your practice. When there, find a comfortable place to lie down, sit or stand. You will need to be in this position for a few minutes, so take a moment to choose a position that supports your comfort. When in position, look around you and find "clues" that tell you that you are in a safe space. After finding a few cues, repeat to yourself quietly, "I am safe right now. I am connected to this world. I am peaceful."

2. Enhance your awareness of your senses. Begin deepening your breath, focusing on long and slow inhales and exhales. Pay attention to how breathing through your nose feels. Identify the subtle movements in your body with each breath. Shift your focus to the sound of your breath. Take a few breaths just listening to the sounds of your inhales and the sounds of your exhale. And now shift your focus again, this time to your awareness of other sensations in your body. Repeat the saying from step one to yourself in your mind, "I am safe right now. I am connected to this world. I am peaceful." If you feel anxiety or any other mental or physical distress, return to step one, looking around you to find the clues that tell your body that you are safe.

3. Experiment with mindfully mobilizing your Vagus nerve. Try by increasing your breathing rate. Move your body. This can include getting into an active yoga posture or walk in swiftly. You can also dance to music. Move just enough to increase your heart rate

and quicken your breath to support you as you move. Repeat the saying again, "I am safe right now. I am connected to this world. I am peaceful." Again, if you are feeling distressed or anxious, return to step one and visually orient yourself back into your safe space.

4. Experiment with mindful immobilization of your Vagus nerve. Now it is time to bring your body back to stillness, whether that is returning to the comfortable position you began in, or by lying down, sitting, or standing still. Encourage your body to be as still as possible and witness your heart rate slowing down. Let your body press firmly into the ground, letting the Earth or the floor hold you. Bring your attention back to breathing deeply and slowly. If you feel comfortable, try extending your exhales to be even longer than your inhales. This helps stimulate the feeling of relaxation. If you are tightening or tensing any muscles, relax them now. Say to yourself quietly, "I am safe right now. I am connected to this world. I am peaceful." If you find yourself anxious or distressed, return to step one to remind yourself that you are in a safe place.

25 Additional Self-guided Healing Exercises

1. Cold temperatures: studies have indicated that when your body has to adjust to colder temperatures, it increases your parasympathetic response system to allow you to relax, thereby inhibiting your sympathetic response. This process is overseen by your Vagus nerve. And this does not need to be an extreme exposure to cold; just a small amount of cold exposure can activate your Vagus nerve. One method you can try is dipping your face in ice-cold water or taking a cold shower. You can also expose yourself to cold by going outside in cold temperatures or standing in front of the open freezer door. Drinking ice-cold water is also effective.

2. Chant or sing. You can easily increase the variability in your heart rate when you sing. You can change this variability in different ways when you sing energetically, sing hymns, chant mantras, or hum. The reason this is effective is because of the stimulation of the vagal pump on your throat. If you sing at the top of your lungs

you can engage the back muscles in your throat, activating your Vagus nerve. It also triggers your sympathetic nervous system along with your Vagus nerve. Also, singing is shown to increase oxytocin production.

3. Practice yoga. Yoga is generally beneficial in increasing activity in the parasympathetic system and activation of your Vagus nerve. In one study participants were either assigned a walking process to help them stabilize their mood and lower anxiety, while another group participated in yoga. Those that participated in yoga had increased levels of thalamic GABA, which was associated with their improved mood, mood stability, and lowered anxiety levels.

4. Practice meditation. Two different "methods" for meditation have been shown to help activate the Vagus nerve, chanting "om," and "loving kindness" guided meditation. Chanting "om," is related to the benefits of singing. "Loving kindness" guided meditation assists in people visualizing a positive and peaceful state. The success of these meditation methods is shown in the measurement of heart rate variability before, during and after meditation.

5. Engaging in positive relationships in social settings. In a study, participants were instructed to meditate. One group was given the mantra to repeat to themselves, "May you feel safe, may you feel happy, may you be healthy, may you live with ease" while visualizing others in a compassionate manner. The other group was given meditation instructions that did not foster a compassionate connection to others. Those that had kind thoughts about other people increased their positive emotions, like hope, peace, amusement, interest, joy, and love. The presence of these increased emotions also correlated with an increase in heart rate variability and a stimulated Vagus nerve.

6. Practice deep and slow breathing techniques. Just taking a few deep breaths can calm you down by stimulating your Vagus nerve. Baroreceptors are in your neck and transmit messages to your brain when your heart rate and blood pressure are too low or too high. When you practice slow and deep breathing you can increase the sensitivity of their receptors and also activate your Vagus nerve. This, in turn, lowers anxiety and blood pressure. An average adult that takes about six breaths in a minute will promote rest and relaxation. As you breathe, focus on ballooning your

stomach out as you inhale, letting the oxygen reach into the lower lobes of your lungs, and as you exhale, pull your navel in to cave in your stomach, pressing out all the oxygen from the lower parts of your lungs. The more dramatic the ballooning and sinking of your stomach, the deeper your breath is on average.

7. Laugh a lot. The more you laugh the more you stimulate your Vagus nerve and calm your body. Studies have shown many times that this really is one of the "best medicines." There are reports where people fainted from laughing too much. This is likely due to overstimulation of the Vagus nerve and the parasympathetic nervous system. The sensation becomes extreme and activates the immobilization response. In addition, people that experience this response to laughter often have an illness called Angelman's, which is a fairly rare condition. It is connected to overstimulation of the Vagus nerve. Also, activation of the Vagus nerve can result in laughter. There are many benefits to laughter in addition to stimulating the Vagus nerve, including lowering the risk of heart disease, improving cognitive functioning, and increasing beta-endorphins.

8. Pray often to your divine source or spiritual guide. Praying to a higher power has shown to activate the Vagus nerve. The studies conducted where on Catholics reciting the rosary prayer in particular; however, it is likely that any prayer to a divine connection can most likely stimulate your Vagus nerve in a similar function. Researchers found that prayer enhanced the rhythm of the heart, improving the resting heart rate as well as the heart rate variability. One observation unique to the study on this reciting the rosary prayer was that the prayer took ten seconds to recite, meaning the participants had to take a breath that lasted for ten seconds, resulting in an average of about six breaths per minute. If you recall earlier, it was explained in the section about breathing exercises that breathing at this slow rate is good for activating your Vagus nerve. It increases your heart rate variability, thereby activating your Vagus nerve.

9. Use PEMF, or magnetic field stimulation. This is something similar to what patients are given to activate a Vagus nerve stimulator that was surgically placed in the body but does not require the surgical intervention in your body. These small devices

send pulses into your body to stimulate the Vagus nerve. You can use them on your digestive tract, neck, and skull. It can help in reducing inflammation, regulate digestion, and improved relaxation.

10. Eat probiotics regularly. The gut is connected to the brain by the Vagus nerve. When your gut is "out of order," it affects your brain. So when you take care of your digestive tract and stomach, you can improve the communication process of the Vagus nerve, and thereby improving the communication of other organs with the brain as well. A study conducted on animals being given a probiotic called Lactobacillus Rhamnosus showed a positive alteration to their GABA levels. These levels are handled by the Vagus nerve.

11. Get in more and better exercise for your body. You do not need to do cross-fit or become a bodybuilder to activate and regulate your Vagus nerve. Just a mild form of exercise can help stimulate your digestion. Digestion is regulated by the Vagus nerve. This means that when you exercise you are stimulating and activating your Vagus nerve, supporting healthy gut function.

12. Get a massage. There are certain areas on your body that connect to your Vagus nerve more superficially. This means that you can access this Vagus nerve easier from the outside of your body. The carotid sinus, tucked in your neck, is known to help stimulate your Vagus nerve. It is easily accessible during a massage. It is known to help prevent and reduce seizures in patients. Using mild and firm pressure during a massage can help stimulate the Vagus nerve. Infant massage is a common therapy parents and caregivers can use to help a baby gain weight. The process stimulates the digestive process, which is regulated and controlled by the Vagus nerve. When the Vagus nerve is stimulated and activated, particularly in the abdominal region, digestion can be improved. Also, massaging your feet can help improve heart rate variability and improve the function on the Vagus nerve. It lowers your heart rate and your blood pressure. All of these benefits are known to lower the risk of developing heart disease.

13. Participate in regular intermittent fasting. This is

an old healing therapy used to help heal many illnesses. Intermittent fasting or reduction in caloric intake can increase your heart rate variability and stimulate your Vagus nerve. There are many studies that show the health benefits of fasting and your well-being. Your metabolism decreases during a fast, which is regulated by your Vagus nerve. Also, your Vagus nerve observes when your blood glucose lowers and your gut's stimuli decreases both chemically and mechanically. Your metabolic rate lowers while your Vagus nerve increases, all because of the impulses transmitted to the brain from your liver. While fasting there is also a decrease in your CRH and CCK, with an increase in NPY, all of which are hormones. But when you eat, everything is flip-flopped. When food is introduced, the signals from your gut increase your sympathetic response. This leads to more stressor responses, such as higher levels of CCK and CRH, and lower levels of NPY. In animal studies, some patients showed that fasting can improve the subdiaphragmatic Vagus nerve activity. Also, fasting increased estrogen receptors in parts of the brain, making you more receptive and sensitive to estrogen, also a link to the Vagus nerve activation.

14. Rest on your right-hand side. There are a few studies that indicate laying or sleeping on your right side helps increase your heart rate variability and activates your Vagus nerve. This is the best side to lay on, while the next best is to lie on your left side. Lying on your back leads to the lowest activation of your Vagus nerve. Resting on this side is directly related to your heart, but also applies appropriate pressure and support of your Vagal response.

15. Gargle liquids. When you activate the back of your throat, you activate your Vagus nerve. This is because the muscles in the back of your throat must contract and release to engage, such as when gargling. This contraction in the back of the throat and these muscles means the Vagus nerve is activated. It also stimulates your digestive tract. You do not need to gargle just mouthwash. You can also practice gargling water any time you take a sip of water before swallowing so that you are constantly engaging, contracting, and activating your Vagus nerves, digestion, and mouth muscles.

16. Eat more seafood, to increase DHA and EPA in

your diet. DHA and EPA are known to lower your heart rate and also increase your heart rate variability. These two "side effects" of these nutrients are evidence that they stimulate your Vagus nerve. The amount of these two nutrients is still uncertain, and more studies are needed to directly correlate the Vagus nerve to the intake of DHA and EPA from seafood, but early evidence suggests it is connected. There are plenty of studies that show the health benefits of these nutrients in other aspects as well as why eating seafood is a good diet decision. Regardless of the lack of scientific evidence for this self-guided exercise, it is still a good health decision.

17. Stimulate the release of oxytocin. When your body releases oxytocin it helps lower your appetite as well as increase relaxation. The levels of this hormone increase when the Vagus nerve is active, sending messages from the digestive tract to the brain. In one study on mice that had their Vagus nerve removed showed that even though the oxytocin was still released, it did not have the same effect on the subjects. For example, the mice without Vagus nerves did not have lowered appetites compared to mice who had a fully functioning Vagus nerve.

18. Increase the amount of zinc you consume. Zinc is a common mineral in foods and in supplements, but surprisingly many humans do not consume enough. In a study where rats were given a diet low or deficient in zinc for three days, it was clear the Vagus nerve was not functioning at full capacity. When zinc was reintroduced the Vagus nerve was activated and stimulated.

19. Use a tongue depressor. This self-guided exercise may sound "hoaky" at first, but think about when you are at the doctor and they use a tongue depressor to check the back of your throat. Do you gag often when they do this? Remember, gagging activates your Vagus nerve! If you are uncertain how to make yourself gag, this is the answer. Combine gagging with singing, and you are effectively "working out" your Vagus nerve, giving it plenty of different stimulation and activation.

20. Go see an acupuncturist. This is not typically something you can do to yourself, but it is something that can make a large difference in the stimulation and function of your Vagus nerve. Thousands of years ago, before they called it the Vagus nerve, practitioners recognized that there are certain points

on the body that stimulate this nerve and that you can access this from small intrusions into the body with needles. One of the most traditional locations for stimulating the Vagus nerve is on the ear. One famous "case" of acupuncture and Vagus nerve stimulation is the death of a man whose heart rate lowered too low during the session.

21. Chew gum. It is like turning on the lights when you chew gum, or complete the action known as CCK. Chewing gum or another substance in a similar manner for an extended period of time allows you to reduce the amount of food you eat in one sitting. This is a reduction in appetite. Your appetite is controlled in part by your Vagus nerve. The Vagus nerve is responsible for sending information from your stomach and digestive tract about your hunger, but CCK reduces this. This is evidence that the Vagus nerve is activated to reduce this craving.

22. Eat a more fibrous diet. If you want to feel fuller and slow down your stomach emptying its contents into your small intestine, you want the Vagus nerve to tell the brain that it is satisfied while eating earlier in the process. To do this, you should increase GLP-1 hormone levels. One of the best ways to do this is to eat more fiber.

23. Give yourself or get a coffee enema. Your Vagus nerve essentially ends in your digestive tract. It plays a large role here and is also easily impacted here. If you are able to increase your bowel, you can increase your activation of the Vagus nerve. One method for increasing your bowel is with an enema.

24. Cough or engage your abdominal muscles. Think about how you feel after having a bowel movement. Most likely your body is more relaxed and you feel "better." The process of having a bowel movement requires you to engage certain muscles with intense and strong activation. This engagement of these muscles helps stimulate your Vagus nerve.

25. Get out in the sunshine. It may sound counter-intuitive given what we know about the harmful rays of the sun and our skin; however, the sun is a good source of MSH or Alpha-MSH. In studies on rats, an introduction of Alpha-MSH helped lower the risk of stroke because of the lowering of inflammation and the activation of the Vagus nerve. In another study, subjects were injected with Alpha-MSH directly into the brain with results

showing moderate activation of the Vagus nerve for some subjects with various conditions. While you cannot inject yourself in the brain with this, you can go sit outside in the sun and let your skin absorb this nutrient for you, engaging your Vagus nerve.

Chapter 6: Healing Exercises for Better Social Functioning

It is common for people to begin negotiating and bargaining in stressful situations. If stress continues, it is common to then become angry and frustrated. The next phase is to shut down. This is related to the more "automatic," or autonomic, nervous system. It is your sympathetic side that tells you to fight, freeze, or run. This is when your Vagus nerve is not activated. Blood flows into your muscles to help you survive. This means the blood moves away from your organs. The other system, your parasympathetic system, is all about relaxation. The idea of "rest and digest" being a nickname for the system is good, but it does not identify the importance of this function.

Your parasympathetic system rules your daily life. Your core functions are controlled by it. All things that come in or exit your body are governed mainly by your parasympathetic system. Long before humans evolved to be what they are today, and before most plant and animal matter existed, organisms had one cell, and were simply focused on bringing in nutrients and expelling waste. All of the evolution between then and today can be traced to these roots. Think about all the things your body does to remove waste and then bring in nutrients; breathing in and out, sweat, excrement and urine, menses, etc. All of these functions are primal and foundational actions necessary for survival. And they are all ruled by the parasympathetic system. This nervous system enlargers your blood vessels to flush out the skin and improve digestion. Birth, growing older, and healing from wounds are also part of this system.

During the process of evolution, beings began to develop legs and arms and other appendages. All designed to help that creature run from or to something else. Maybe the being now wanted to chase new food sources, or it needed to run from other creatures chasing it to eat it. This new development created a new nervous system in the body, the sympathetic nervous system. Now your blood moves less quickly, reserving it for later, and metabolism slows to conserve energy sources. It moves blood and other nutrients from the organs in the body and redirects it to muscles and these new limbs to encourage movement.

Your body activates the sympathetic system when it is stressed. But your body is not designed to stay in this stressful state. It is meant to enter it to either eliminate the threat or escape it. And when the moment passes, the body returns to the parasympathetic system's functioning. The problem is that now you do not live with real bears and dinosaurs chasing you, but with mental ones. Think about the job that you hate going to, the bad relationship you are suffering, the messaging on media channels about all the doom and destruction across the globe, etc. All of these provide stress to your body and keep it in this state because the stressors never seem to go away. There are many medical professionals who spend their days trying to get people to get out of this state. These professionals spend a lot of time talking about how important it is to "avoid" this sympathetic state. But in reality, you do not want to avoid it, just minimize it, or find a balance between the two.

Some doctors have discovered and published information about how to keep cardiac patients from relapsing or returning to the hospital. During their study and observation, patients were observed during cardiac rehabilitation. It is well known that operating in a high-stress, parasympathetic state for a long time can lead to the system eventually "wearing out." The functions necessary to keep your internal organs functioning begin to malfunction. Think about your heartbeat. You know your heart is beating fast because messages from your nerves triggered in the parasympathetic system; however, if those nerves become worn out, you may not recognize or be able to control your fast heart rate. But those that operated only in the parasympathetic state, not experiencing any stress for a long period of time, also had problems with the fading of their vital organ function, but in a different manner.

The evidence of this shows that an easy and peaceful body is not solely reliant upon a dominant parasympathetic system all the time. Think of it like cylinders; if you have two cylinders, but only fire from one, eventually that cylinder is going to burn out. There are consequences to "firing" from only one nervous system and not both. Like a car and its cylinders, if the body does this, it will begin to shut down and may even die. For organisms that still have one cell, the feigning of death is a survival technique. If that organism feared a situation, they appear to be dead. A human can respond primitively in a similar manner, as outlined earlier in this book. Some of those primitive responses include crying, attention-seeking, and silence. Think about the "silent treatment." It is a form of shutting down socially to alert the social threat of the other person. In a sense, you are "playing dead" until the threat is either extinguished or removed. But sometimes this response goes too far and ends up damaging your mind and/or body.

Friendships and rekindling old relationships are the "key" to helping cardiac patients during rehab. And it is a lesson that can easily be applied in your daily life, healthy heart or not.

Part of the polyvagal theory explored earlier in this book in Chapter 4, is what some people call the "social nerve system." Dr. Stephen Porges developed this concept, going on to describe how the social nerve system is a portion of the brain where the eyes, voice, and facial expressions are influenced and are used to influence others. The reason babies are so often used as examples for this theory is that human babies are born helpless. They need protection and support as they continue to develop. Because they cannot walk or talk, the infant human body adapted with skills designed to activate the social nerve system in the adult. While modern science may still only recognize or discuss two nervous systems, the sympathetic and parasympathetic, there is a third that needs to be injected into the system that offers an explanation to the gaps that still exist when it is just the two polarities. Each one of the systems is designed to deal with stress in a different manner. For example, think of an infant who shifts its body to face toward their parent, and uses their eyes and facial gestures to signal his or her parents. If this fails and no one acknowledges the message she or he is trying to send, the parasympathetic nervous system is activated and the infant begins to get angry and cry. And if this message still goes unanswered, the infant can then "play dead," becoming quiet and still. As the infant learns how the different responses and strategies work, the more it becomes ingrained in their subconscious and used as they grow into an adult.

This third system, the social nervous system, makes sense. The entire body and mind, including your nervous system, seeks balance inside and out. It wants to not only be harmonious in its internal functioning, but it also wants to feel harmonious with its surroundings. This is why, when your life is stressful and "stormy," you probably have a natural tendency or inclination to reach out to someone to find empathy. You want or even need to share with others because it is important for your survival to know that you are not alone and that what you are going through is not just a "you" thing or something that sets you apart from the rest.

With this information now in your "tool belt," you may feel like a fog has dissipated and you can finally see yourself and others more clearly now. Now that you know the social nervous system and the three systems and responses, you can recognize the stage a person is in. Not only does this help you, but it helps you see how other people are doing around you. Are they shutting down and "playing dead" because you or others have failed to acknowledge their needs? Or are they screaming for attention? Can you try and catch them when they are engaging their social nervous system and displaying the polyvagal theory in their facial expressions?

Your body and brain send out various energetic frequencies. Think about brain waves. These are like sound waves and are measurable frequencies. Researchers, such as Dr. Joe Dispenza, identified that infant brain waves are primal and connected to the development of the subconscious. During this time the subconscious is being developed and finalized with the important survival needs. It is developing a strategy to help you survive as you grow and later in life. When the infant reaches childhood, the brain waves and frequencies shift. They become more creative. Imagination and creative play, like turning an everyday object into a monster, dinosaur or horse. It is also why monsters live under the bed, etc.

These frequencies do not leave you when you become an adult, but often they become only active right before and just as you fall asleep. It is also common just when you wake up or when you are deep in meditation. These connections are very close to the subconscious. In these states, you have the ability to change the pattern of your neurology and "reprogram" what you learned as an infant and young child about survival among other things.

When you turn ten your brainwaves and energetic frequencies change again. Now they are more "mature" and follow a more rational approach. This change continues throughout adulthood. At this point the brain can identify the difference between different things, like the everyday object is not really a dinosaur and the shadow is just a shadow, not a monster. In addition, it provides the ability to rationalize emotions and situations. For example, you can find a rational reason why you should not deal with your emotions. But while you may convince your mind not to deal with it, eventually it will come out, and your body will respond in ways you cannot or do not want to control. You rationalize yourself into illness.

At this point, you have learned about the various stages of brain and energy waves, as well as the three nervous systems; social, sympathetic, and parasympathetic. You have also been introduced to the idea that the way adults respond to stressful situations, in particular, is due to the strategies they found which worked best for them when they were children. From a neuroscience point of view, this information is transformational. This information shows that the immune system, endocrine, and nervous system are all connected and working together inside you.

The concept is basic; if you are socially unable to cope with your stress, the body then begins to "fight, flight, or freeze." This physiological state is not a place you want or should stay in long. If you do not cope with this threat or stress quickly, your body and mind start to fade. How you choose to interact with others includes the degree of interaction as well as the manner of contact. This determines the majority of your health. To find this balance and harmony, you need to do more than just meditate for 15 minutes every day by yourself or do a 30-minute relaxation yoga video by yourself. This is why the third system, the social nervous system, regulated largely by the Vagus nerve, supports your need to connect. Think about the importance of going to church on a Saturday or Sunday. You can pray at home but it is important to be together with others that support your view on spirituality. It is also why going to a fitness class is a far different outcome, especially on your happiness, than doing a program at the house by yourself. This means it is not about the actions physically, but about the connection socially. Studies at this stage people's brain waves become calmer and more peaceful. And all of this knowledge then leads to a powerful change agent you can use in your future.

Anxiety, Social Situations, and the Vagus Nerve

In Latin, the term "vagus" is a derivative of the word "vagabond." A vagabond is considered a wanderer, a person who travels is a loose fashion. While the Vagus nerve is not necessarily loose and meandering without purpose, it is still a nerve that travels around the body for a long time. It is like a river, the course of it moving from one place to the next, but with a direction and purpose. The purpose of the Vagus nerve is to communicate sensations to the brain. It is born in the brainbox, housed inside the spinal column at the base of your skull. It descends through your neck, wandering into the pharynx, larynx, esophagus, trachea, and bronchi. It branches into the lungs and heart, before coursing down into the stomach, pancreas, and liver. It communicates the messages from the brain to these places. But in addition, it listens to what is happening to the various organs and places that it passes by and sends that all back to the brain. This communication between a large majority of your body and your brain gets interesting.

There is a strong relationship between emotions and the Vagus nerve, as seen in Chapter 2 of this book. The Vagus is responsible for sending signals back forth about the emotional state of the body, including if it is relaxed, calm, angry, or anxious. As explored in previous chapters, there are two parts to the Vagus nerve that have different roles and are equally important. These two polar opposite parts are both responsible for telling the brain what is going on in your body. Here comes the parasympathetic and sympathetic nervous system that communicates stress or relaxation to the brain. But as explained earlier in this chapter, there is a third part to the nervous system that deals with the description of the social function of your body and brain.

All three systems have gas and brakes, essentially. And the messages sent to the body when the "gas pedal" is pushed determine how your brain responds to the environment and situation you are in. Think about when you are facing a bear. Your sympathetic system "floors the gas" to tell your body to move. This causes the other systems to slam on their brakes and let the sympathetic system drive for a bit. But the sympathetic system is like a young driver with a lot of road rage. It is wild and sometimes uncontrollable. It is not safe to let this system drive for a long time. But they sure are great at getting you away from trouble! The other two systems have their own drive and impact. For example, the parasympathetic kicks in when the danger is passed and the body can relax now. This system "takes the wheel" and begins slowing things down, getting back on the road, and following the road rules. To communicate in this manner, there are neurotransmitters spread throughout the body by the Vagus nerve. One such neurotransmitter, for example, is acetylcholine. This is designed to tell the heart to slow down and the bread pressure to lower in an effort to slow down the function of your other organs as well.

Most of this information has been shared before in this book; however, it is important that you remember how the Vagus nerve engages in several different functions in the body and how communication happens between organs and your brain. Your Vagus nerve is both highway and driver. Your organs and brain are simply the starting and ending points. Some of the functions that the Vagus nerve engages in or creates includes:

- Heartbeat regulation
- Breathing muscle movement and pace of breath
- Intestine and stomach muscle contractions to allow for food

digestion

- Digestion tract maintenance
- Stimulates relaxation after a stressful event to alert the body the danger has passed
- Tells the brain information gathered by your senses regarding the state of various vital organs.

Anxiety and Your Vagus Nerve

When you are in stressful situations, you activate your sympathetic nervous system. In an ideal situation, and how your body has evolved to respond best, the stress will dissipate and your body activates the parasympathetic nervous system to relax again. But sometimes this does not happen at all or within a healthy time frame. This means your body continues to respond in a heightened, stressful state, and now problems start to manifest. From a neurological standpoint, two things begin to happen:

1. Activation of the brain-intestine axis
2. Activation of the hypothalamus-pituitary-adrenal axis

Your brain feels stressed for a long time and anxious so it creates more hormones, or CRF's. These start in the hypothalamus and then travel to your pituitary gland. Here they create another hormone to release into your body, ACTH. This moves from the pituitary to the bloodstream and finally off to the adrenal glands. Once here, the influx of hormones triggers adrenaline and cortisol production. This creation is what suppresses your immune system function and precursors to inflammation. This explains why when you are suffering from anxiety and chronic stress, you can get sick easier. This can ultimately end in depression. This is a disorder many have linked to the brain's response of inflammation.

But there is more than happens when the body is suffering from anxiety and chronic stress. Your body also increases glutamate in your brain. This is another neurotransmitter that can cause symptoms such as migraines, more anxiety, and depression, especially in excessive levels. Increased levels of cortisol also shrink the physical volume of your hippocampus. This is the section of your brain responsible for forming new memories. You now have a smaller area to be able to do this effectively.

Stimulating the Vagus nerve for too long in this manner can result in physical responses such as challenges breathing, heartbeat irregularities, GI tract issues, and dizziness. You can also face emotional challenges, such as extreme emotions that can appear or feel uncontrollable. As the system remains in the sympathetic nervous system for a length of time, the body and response system becomes more impulsive. And you can then suffer from severe anxiety.

A recent study from the University of Miami has shown that a mother's vagal tone is communicated with their fetus. If the mother is struggling with anger, depression or anxiety, their vagal tone is lowered. When their child is born, there is a lower level of serotonin and dopamine as well as a lower vagal tone as well. The connection is undeniable; if a pregnant woman is suffering from these "threatening" emotions, their unborn child will as well.

The best way to treat this situation is to prevent your body from remaining in this state, or learning how to stimulate your Vagus nerve and allow your body to "override" the sympathetic response. You need to care for your Vagus nerve and keep it acting properly so you can "slam on the brakes" of fight, flight, or freeze, and let yourself relax.

Remember, your vagal tone is a biological process that identifies the Vagus nerve's activity levels. Increasing your vagal tone means increasing your relaxation. Your Parasympathetic system is activated and you can "handle" stress a lot easier. This positively impacts the balance of your emotions and general well-being.

Chapter 7: The Vagus Nerve and Autism

Not only does your body help you deal with stressful and threatening situations, but it also helps you empathize with others and communicate socially. It deals with sensory, motor, and emotional information. It is critical in your overall health and well-being. Things like your organ function, your brain, your health, and your emotional responses are all controlled or influenced by your Vagus nerve. It is incredible how much it is connected and vital in your daily life.

The two branches of your Vagus nerve break out from the brainstem and travel around, touching various points, and collect and send the important details back to the brain to be deciphered. When this nerve is underdeveloped or under-active, it can be a major cause for autistic symptoms. It impacts the autonomic or "automatic" responses in your body, meaning it is not something you can control consciously. These responses are connected to the functions necessary for your survival. Think about breathing, your heart pumping, digestion, etc. It is within these "automatic" responses that your body choose one of the three systems to call upon, the social nervous system, sympathetic nervous system, and parasympathetic nervous system. So, if your subconscious system is connected to these automatic responses to stress and calm, it can be hard to imagine how it is possible to impact them. They happen at a level that cannot be controlled by conscious thought. Your Vagus nerve is the answer. This nerve controls almost all of how your body responds to your senses. It determines if it is a threat or not and if your body should empathize, mobilize, or be still.

Previously in this book, you were introduced to the Polyvagal theory. This concept introduced by Steven Porges, a researcher at the University of Illinois, was the one to explain the three various nervous systems that respond to stress automatically. These autonomic functions developed over the course of thousands or millions of years and allow you to not only primitively respond but also respond socially. The three systems Porges identified are:

1. **Unmyelinated Vagus Nerve:** If it is not possible to remove yourself from the threatening situation, your most basic and primitive response is triggered. It is like animals that become paralyzed when afraid, like turtles or sharks. It is like playing dead or fainting when scared or overly stressed. A turtle is startled and

it pulls into its shell. An opossum is startled and it plays dead. These are all unmyelinated Vagus nerve responses.
   2. **Sympathetic Nervous System:** When a threat is perceived, the body "overrides" the restful and peaceful state of your body to get it ready to move. Cortisol is secreted, which is the hormone necessary for being able to fight off an attack or run from it.
   3. **Myelinated Vagus Nerve:** This is the most evolved nervous system for mammals. It is operating when you do not perceive a threat around you. It holds back the more primitive responses and creates an environment for social interaction. You can use this higher-operating state to decide is a person is a friend or someone you do not want to be around. It also helps you determine if a certain environment is safe for you or not. This system promotes social communication and connection.

Numerous studies and years of research show how valid this theory applies to the human condition today. Now more researchers, scientists, and medical professionals are using this information to help them create new therapies for various patients suffering from illnesses like rheumatoid arthritis and epilepsy.

Autism is an underactive Vagus nerve. The body does not send signals that are strong enough to the brain, so the autonomic functions are impaired. When the Vagus nerve cannot do its job as it has evolved to do in modern mammals, the dominant nervous system is parasympathetic. This is a chronic state of stress and "fight, flight, or freeze." As a result, many patients diagnosed with autism face side effects, such as health issues and behavioral imbalances commonly associated with autism.

The emotions, love, and empathy, are absent for reptiles that are non-mammalian and more primitive. These two emotions, in particular, allow mammals and especially humans to be social and live together in groups peacefully. It also is what allows you to see and respond to social cues, communicate with one another effectively, create emotional bonds with another person, and work with one another. It is why humans can nurture a child from infancy for many years, raising them to then pass on that empathy and love to others. A fully functioning Vagus nerve is what allows humans to live together in a social setting by offering the neurological support to make it happen. In addition to the social aspect, the Vagus nerve regulates things like your digestion, heart rate, and breathing. It is the Vagus nerve that can tell the body it is time to relax and be at peace when something stressful triggered it.

Think back to all the things that the Vagus nerve controls; hearing, sight, social responsiveness, emotions, heart rate, digestion, etc. It even is responsible for triggering the increase, creation or release of various hormones like oxytocin, your "feel good" hormone, vasopressin, and acetylcholine. It signals your digestive tract to secrete intrinsic factor and pepsin. It controls a lot of what makes you function at a high level.

The method the Vagus nerve uses to do this is to interpret sensory receptors. For example, what you smell, hear, see, or touch all is delivered to the brain. Even your balance and sense of physical pressure is interpreted. The signals run up the spinal nerve roots to the spinal cord. This is a direct shot to the low brain or the cerebellum. It is like food to the cerebellum. This "food" or information is then "digested" and turned into a response. Whatever the message about the environment, the brain sends a response.

Many years ago, medical professionals thought the movement was coordinated by your cerebellum. Now it is clear that the cerebellum actually controls impulse behaviors and thoughts. When the signals are sent to the cerebellum, they move then to the outside film of neural tissue found in humans called the brain cortex. Here the information increases the firing frequency, causing stimulation to "workout" the brain. It keeps your brain healthy and viable. When this stimulation does not occur your brain loses the active control over primal function. This includes loss of subconscious control over things like regulating pain and breathing.

Several of the symptoms of autism occur at the brain stem, the place of origin for the Vagus nerve. It is the source of malfunction if you will. When the cortex does not receive the input necessary from your cerebellum your brain becomes incapable of controlling the rest of the brain stem functioning. If the Vagus nerve is underactive the mid-brain becomes more uncontrolled and overactive. Your cranial nerve functions are imbalanced. Then, the imbalance develops distortions for the senses. Some of these include light sensitivity, or photophobia, sound distortion, pressure on the inner ear, dizziness, fatigue, systemic pain, heart arrhythmia, and issues with digestion. The Vagus nerve is evolved to help prevent your body from becoming overly stimulated, but when it is underactive, your mid-brain becomes overactive to compensate.

Symptoms of Autism and Your Vagus Nerve

The underactivity of your Vagus nerve, your longest cranial nerve starting from your brainstem and leading to your colon, is now the likely cause of the symptoms of illnesses like fibromyalgia, chronic fatigue, and autism. It is an interesting observation for many years that mothers who have children with autism often suffer from illnesses such as fibromyalgia or chronic fatigue. What is now theorized and being researched more is the likelihood of these two diseases actually being autism that came on in adulthood. It is also the explanation for why more people with diabetes also have autism. The Vagus nerve is responsible for regulating the production and secretion of insulin in the body, and a failure to respond or produce enough is linked to the proper function of the Vagus nerve.

Another observation is that many people with celiac also have autism. Celiac, or an allergy to gluten, is founded in the gut. Your Vagus nerve controls the gut. If your digestion is not operating properly and is slower than average, most likely the Vagus nerve is not functioning properly. Your intestinal lining likely becomes damaged and maldigestion occurs most likely because of a highly inflammatory substances in genetically modified foods, such as gliadin in wheat. This damage causes a disruption to your Vagus nerve, causing illness to inflammatory foods, such as gluten. People with autism often suffer from infections in their intestines. Your immune system and your digestion are both stimulated or suppressed by your Vagus nerve response. If you are not digesting your food properly and it begins to develop pathogens like Klebsiella, Clostridia, or yeast, you become sick.

There are several things that can impair the proper function of your Vagus nerve. The root cause of many people with fibromyalgia, chronic fatigue, and autism includes the viral infection of the Vagus nerve, HHV-6, or Human Herpesvirus 6. This is a chronic infection located in the Vagus nerve itself that possibly leads to a chronic state of impaired function for mitochondria. It potentially also impairs your immune function, creates issues with your digestion, and leads to the distortion of your senses. There is a virus that potentially impairs the Vagus nerve as well. Two such viruses that can cause an infection in the Vagus nerve are Cytomegalovirus and Epstein-Barr. In addition, if there is a high level of mercury in the body and it leads to mercury poisoning, acetylcholine action can become blocked. This is the neurotransmitter the Vagus nerve uses to send sensory signals and information to the body from the brain.

One symptom of autism is spinning. Many people are curious about the reason for this response, and for many years medical professionals were unsure of the reason, offering a variety of theories. One reason for the spinning response is because it is a form of Vagus nerve stimulation. An underactive Vagus nerve can make the body feel that it is off-balance, and spinning helps stimulate the nerve and tell the brain it is more balanced. In many people with autism, spinning is a therapeutic response. It is a way to help those with autism better orientate themselves to their space. It can also assist in developing the system for balance in the body, which is the lead integration for the additional senses in the human body.

Another symptom of autism is flapping of their hands. This is another action designed to stimulate the Vagus nerve. Like spinning, it helps orient the body. It helps regulate the Vagus nerve. The feedback you receive from the senses in your extremities is essential for orienting you in your page. It lets you recognize the space your body takes up, where it "ends" and where the outside environment begins. For those with autism that lack proper feedback from their senses in their extremities, or proprioceptive feedback, they often struggle with feeling out of place in their environment and not fully understanding who they are and are not compared to their environment around them. This includes other people. This explanation is helpful in understanding why orientation and relaxation occur when the body is gently pressured from all around, like when using the Temple Grandin "squeeze machine." This pressure regulates and stimulates the Vagus nerve which in turn helps calm the body and mind and allows a person the opportunity to orient to their space. Think about a frantic infant and how a warm and firm hug or tight swaddle can help the baby become more peaceful. It is an instinct in mothers, and most adults, to hug or wrap someone up when they are operating in a primitive state. Infants are great examples of how an immature Vagus nerve can be stimulated with "treatments" like pressure and the "squeeze machine." The neurotransmitters are calmed down and the body and mind respond in like.

Speech is a challenge for many with autism. Not only do people with autism have speech delays but they can also display difficulty in understanding speech. This is because of the ability to hear and listen. The action of listening requires the contraction or tension of the middle ear. It is considered a motor action. The muscles in your middle ear are also responsible for regulating things like your eyelids lifting up and your facial nerves. Consider what your face does when someone tells you something interesting. Your eyelids lift, maybe even your eyebrows. When this happens the muscles in your middle ear are tensing. Even when the environment is noisy, this action actually helps you be able to listen to their voice better. It is like you have a built-in noise cancellation system to allow you to hear only the information from the speaker you are interested in. But those with autism may not have this. The tone of his or her middle ear may not be sufficient and cannot block out that external or background noise. This not only makes it hard to hear the other person but also hard to look at them. In addition, there is a time lag when someone is processing auditory information for some people who have autism. This means that the sound is playing in the movie of their mind just a little bit after the "actors" have said something. It is like the whole world is just a little bit out of sync. The images this person sees does not match the sounds they are hearing, and it is confusing, frustrating, and disorienting.

When you are watching a movie where the audio is just a little "off," have you ever tried looking away from the screen and just listening to the sound? Did it feel a little less strange and a bit more enjoyable? Some people with autism do not like or cannot make eye contact with other people. One of the reasons is maybe because of this auditory lag. Another reason may be because the eye gaze, which is spontaneous in most humans, is switched off in the neural system. If you feel unsafe in a situation or space, you are not able to make eye contact easily. The more developed nervous system response of social engagement is only activated when the body feels at ease and secure. People with autism do not operate in this state often or at all, making eye contact either hard or more likely impossible.

When the body is sick, function levels change, often to be more aligned with a fully functioning Vagus nerve. This occurs in almost 50% of patients with autism. When a person who responds this way gets a fever, their body switches systems. It is now operating in a metabolic state. These are systems engaged when the Vagus nerve is functioning at full capacity. This is why people with autism often show improvements in their functioning when they are sick and have a fever. And it is likely you will see people with autism sick more often than others. This is because they have a lower immune system. They are more prone to infection. The simple explanation is that the Vagus nerve is responsible for stimulating your immune system. It is meant to tell your body to fight off the infection but if the Vagus nerve is not functioning at proper levels, it cannot tell your body to fight, allowing the infection to materialize.

In addition to your immune system and your gut, the Vagus nerve tells the body how to regulate its toxicity when food sources are ingested. But again, in those with underactive Vagus nerves, like those with autism, this can lead to a build-up of heavy metals and toxins. This can then lead to heavy metal poisoning and additional symptoms and illnesses. Moving down into the intestine, the Vagus nerve is important to the stimulation of the small intestine's intrinsic factor production. This makes B12 for your body. But those with autism often have low levels or deficiencies in B12. Stimulating the Vagus nerve can help readjust this temporarily.

Moving back up, consider the speech of those with autism and how many speak in a unique modulation and have various enunciations for words. This is primarily due to the Vagus nerve and its role in the stimulation of the larynx. These muscles are necessary for the ability of speech, and when impaired the person cannot speak "properly." Hearing, also controlled and influenced by the Vagus nerve, is connected to the person's ability to speak and enunciate correctly. If the person has trouble hearing the words correctly, they are then unable to speak correctly because they do not understand the difference in sound. Often, they are mimicking the sounds that they hear in their speech. Many of the muscles in the face and head are impacted by the Vagus nerve. This includes the muscles in your face that allow for facial animation. If there is a breakdown in communication between the face and the rest of the body with the brain, it is common for the face to lack animation. People with autism may not appear to feel a certain way or have a certain emotion because their face is not capable of expressing it. One of the most common locations for a lack of expression is from the nose level and higher. The eyes do not lift up and down with interest. The eyebrows do not furrow or raise. The forehead does not wrinkle in concern. All of this fails to occur because the Vagus nerve is failing to do its job.

These are some of the many reasons for additional research and study into the role of the Vagus nerve and autism. Many of the symptoms of people with autism can be explained with a malfunction of the Vagus nerve, meaning therapies to stimulate and activate the nerve can be effective in treating those with autism.

Chapter 8: Helping Others Find Proper Vagus Nerve Function

Many people have no idea what the Vagus nerve is. They do not realize it is the tenth cranial nerve and is also the longest cranial nerve in the body. But beyond that, they do not realize how complex it is. It can be hard to fathom, as you may have experienced at the beginning of this book, all the functions of this nerve. It is incredible the information "highway" this nerve provides from several organs to your brain, and back. It may not look like this nerve has a specific purpose or direction, because of its wandering appearance; however, it has evolved to do very specific tasks at very specific locations in a precise manner.

The nerve itself has many cell bodies for sensory nerve cells. These are organized into two "bundles." While there are technically two Vagus nerves, it is considered or referred to as one nerve. The bundles of sensory nerve bodies begin at the base of the skull at the brain stem and are essentially the connection of the brain to the body. Your brain sends and receives information here. The functions of this nerve are described and researched in detail. It is "broken" into different nervous systems that it provides; however, one of the most prominent and most popular for discussion is the autonomic nervous system, which has the social, sympathetic, and parasympathetic nervous systems, or functions, within it. It controls or influences directly a large variety of sensory responses as well as motor activities. In a nutshell, it is a "string" tied to the abdomen, lungs, heart, and neck connected and "hanging" from the brain. There is a good reason many people either do not know about, are confused by, or overwhelmed by what the Vagus nerve is and what it does!

Help Others Know About the Vagus Nerve

First, you should let other people learn about the role and importance of their Vagus nerve before launching into therapies and techniques they can use for balancing and stimulating theirs. To help introduce all there is about the Vagus nerve, you can explain the following:

- The longest nerve created in the brain that extends through your neck, lungs, heart, and abdomen.
- Sends information from the body to the brain and back from the

brain to the body.
- This nerve is responsible for your automatic responses to stressful situations, such as your "fight, flight or freeze" response or your ability to relax and be calm.

Once you set the foundation of what the nerve is, you can set up the functions of the nerve for deeper understanding. Explain to others the four primary functions of the Vagus nerve:

1. Parasympathetic: Controls your heart rate rhythm, breathing, and digestion.
2. Motor: Influences motor functions in the neck specifically related to speech and swallowing.
3. Sensory: Gathers information from the sensory receptors related to the abdomen, lungs, heart, and throat.
4. Unique sensory: Stimulates the sensations behind the tongue responsible for taste.

There are additional functions; however, these are the four primaries. And within these, they can be further divided into seven parts. One of the parts of this is to keep your nervous system balanced. The nervous system is something many people are used to experiencing; however, may not know a lot about or what it really does. You can help break this down for others by highlighting the following:

- Social Nervous System
- Sympathetic Nervous System
- Parasympathetic Nervous System

The two most commonly referenced and talked about are the sympathetic and parasympathetic systems. The sympathetic system is about mobility and action. You become more alert, have more energy, blood pressure increases, heart rate speeds up, and breathing becomes quicker. The parasympathetic system is the opposite. It encourages rest and stillness. It lowers the alertness of the body, blood pressure lowers, heart rate is your "resting" rate, digestion is regular, and the body, in general, feels calm and relaxed. In this state, the body can stabilize and experience things like sexual arousal, urination, and defecation.

And while these functions are some of the most commonly referenced in terms of the Vagus nerve, there are other functions that are interesting and important for people to know:

- The gut and brain talk through the Vagus nerve. Because the Vagus nerve is in the stomach and digestive tract, if there is anything off or imbalanced in the gut, the brain knows about it from the Vagus nerve.
- Deep breathing helps you relax thanks to the Vagus nerve. Your diaphragm communicates with the brain by the Vagus nerve. When the diaphragm is able and engaging in deep breathing it is a cue to the brain that there is no immediate threat and it can relax. The brain gets this cue from the Vagus nerve.
- Inflammation is lowered. When the body is relaxed it does not need inflammation to "protect" it like it can respond with when threatened. This especially happens when the body fears a threat from inside and begins increasing chronic inflammation, causing a host of health issues over time. If the Vagus nerve recognizes that the body is not threatened, internally or externally, it sends signals to the various parts of your body to reduce the levels of inflammation. This is turn helps "cure" chronic inflammation and bring the body back to balance and well-being.
- Blood pressure and heart rate become lowered and regulated. Getting blood to circulate in the body is the job for the heart. But if the heart does not know how much or how fast to pump the blood, there can be major problems. For example, damage to your organs and loss of consciousness is possible. The heart learns what the body needs from the Vagus nerve. If the nerve is not functioning properly it can tell the heart to slow down too slow so blood is not making it around the body, or it does not regulate it enough to keep it from pumping too fast.
- Manage your fear. The reason you feel emotions in your "gut" is because of the Vagus nerve. When you are scared, anxious, or stress, the Vagus nerve interprets these signals in the gut and sends the information to the brain from there. This is why you have a "gut feeling" that something is not right, or get a stomach ache when you get stressed out or scared.
- Despite all the knowledge researched and published on this nerve,

there is still more to do. There are still many questions that are left unanswered or revelations that need to be confirmed. This is why there are still many studies being conducted on this nerve and its function in the body. For example, can Vagus never stimulation help treat a variety of illnesses and conditions in the body because it is a direct link between it and the brain.

Some of the conditions being researched in connection to the Vagus nerve include:

- Crohn's Disease and inflammation caused by it
- Heart rhythm abnormalities
- Hiccups that are intractable
- Diabetes mellitus and chronic inflammation caused by it
- Heart failure
- Rheumatoid arthritis and inflammation related to it

For those suffering from rheumatoid arthritis, which is about 1.3 million American adults, one promising study published in 2016 showed that stimulation of the Vagus nerve could help reduce the symptoms of the condition. For people suffering from this condition but did not respond to other therapies for it found that they had significant improvements when their Vagus nerve was stimulated. In addition, no negative side effects were reported. This study, in particular, is a "breakthrough" in understanding how the stimulation of the Vagus nerve can be used in the treatment of various conditions. Additional conditions being researched include Alzheimer's and Parkinson's, as well as Crohn's disease, as mentioned earlier.

Now that you describe this to another person in a simple breakdown such as this, you can get into the details of how you can help him or her stimulate their Vagus nerves for optimal health and function. Many of these methods described in this chapter are similar to the self-guided methods and suggestions throughout this book; however, they are adapted to be applicable to a guide for you to help someone else. You will not be able to insert a device into the body along the Vagus nerve to stimulate it with a mechanical pump unless you are a medical professional with proper training in the process. But you can manually stimulate with a variety of things, like a handheld device that delivers electrical pulses into the body along the nerve. It is especially effective behind the ear.

A Helpful Guide for Helping Others

Below are nine techniques you can help others learn and use in their life to stimulate and balance their Vagus nerve. The nine techniques include:

1. Deep breathing exercises from the diaphragm
2. Physical activity levels each day
3. Connecting socially face to face
4. Journaling in an expressive and narrative manner
5. Self-talk in the third person with positive messaging
6. Promotion of the "small" self through the sense of wonder
7. Conducting a loving-kindness meditation to help lift the mood and connectivity
8. Transcendent ecstasy in a secular and superfluid way
9. Altruistic preparation for the next generation and volunteering in the community for the benefit of future generations

Deep Breathing Exercises from Your Diaphragm and Your Vagus Nerve

"Slow abdominal breathing" is a method used for relaxation for thousands of years. You can do this any time and in any place. It is an instant stimulation for your Vagus nerve. It is a technique sages and yoga practitioners have used for thousands or millions of years in Eastern culture. They have known that breathing from the diaphragm is essential to overall well-being, and they even recognized that it stimulated their body in some fashion, despite not knowing directly about the Vagus nerve at the time.

Later, in the 1970s, leaders in the mind-body field, Jon Kabat-Zinn and Herbert Benson popularized the breathing technique, explaining how the process balances the body by impacting your autonomic nervous system. Now it is widely accepted by Western medical professionals today as an effective method for this stimulation, helping the body become calm. You can find hundreds if not thousands of scholarly and medical studies published regarding the effectiveness of deep breathing from the diaphragm.

In addition to being a technique you can teach to others to be used any time and any place, there are no real "rules" regarding how to do it. If a person just begins to breathe as deeply as they can, they are doing well. There are tips for doing it different ways to encourage deeper breathing that you can pass along as well.

1. Imagine you are filling up your abdomen with air like a balloon. Fill it as full as you can make it, and then slowly let all the air out by tucking in your belly button under your ribcage.
2. Breathe as slowly as you can filling your lungs from the bottom to the top, lifting your collar bones when the air reaches the top. Let the air out just as slowly, emptying from the top until the very bottom.
3. Focus on a slow inhale, but an even slower exhale. Count how many seconds it takes to fully breathe in, and then try to double the amount of time it takes to inhale on your exhale.
4. Breathe in slowly through your mouth, not your nose. Then try it only breathing through your nose. Observe which method makes you feel more relaxed, safe, and calm. Whatever method makes you feel this way, spend a few moments doing that. You can also alternate breathing in through your nose and out through your mouth, or vice versa.

You do not need to do this exercise every day but you can make time for it regularly. It is a great tool for those that feel a stressful response in their body, or the activation of the sympathetic system, and want to calm it back down. Either way, it is effective and beneficial to the body. Thankfully, there are no "wrong" ways to breathe, so whether you are doing it "right" or "wrong," as long as you are breathing you are doing well. It is important to keep in mind that when you are in a stressed and sympathetic state, you do not feel like you have the time to slow down and take deep breaths if you think of the technique at all. This is why having a daily practice can help in making sure you have practice and dedicated time to do it for your healthy mind and body.

Physical Activity Levels Each Day

Physical activity, in particular, aerobic activity, is a known stimulus of the Vagus nerve. It helps lower your stress levels and encourage your body to return to a relaxed state. Your HRV, or heart rate variability, is improved with various vigorous, moderate, and low levels of physical activity. There is an important caveat with this Vagus nerve stimulation: physical activity is good only if you feel good after. If you work out too rigorously you can actually end up lowering your HRV and reduce your vagal tone. You go beyond a healthy level and end up harming yourself instead. This is possibly one of the largest areas of assistance you can provide to another, recognizing that there is a limit and helping them respect their limit. This also means that for one person, vigorous activity is necessary to their Vagus nerve stimulation, while for another they need low or moderate levels. In addition, the level of exertion may be perceived differently for one person versus another. This is called "Rate Perceived Exertion," or RPE. One person may feel that their exertion is far greater performing one exercise while another feels it is not as great to them.

There is controversy still over what the "best" level of exercise is for a person's well-being. The reality is; however, that we are programmed to avoid painful situations and seek pleasure. If exercising becomes painful or disagreeable, chances are it will be avoided. This is called the "pleasure principle" and is important in the success of an exercise program. If the workout is enjoyable, it is more likely to occur again and make you feel better than a more intense but less enjoyable situation. If you approach, or encourage someone else to approach, exercise with pleasure in mind, the level of activity will naturally vary from one moment to the next, in addition to changing with age, but will be more likely to persist over time than if sticking to a formula that is no longer "fun."

Determining if you are exercising enough can be measured in your heart rate variability, of HRV. Technically, this requires you to use an advanced tool to find out, but there are other options that can help track your heart rate. These can measure the RR intervals. These include tools like those manufactured by FitBit, LifeTrak, Mio Alpha, and Polar. What these all have in common is the information they share. The information provided by the tool is your own unique heart rate. The challenge is that your heart rate will be different than just about anyone else in the world. You cannot and should not compare your heart rate to anyone else's. Use your monitor for a few weeks to find a baseline or average heart rate. Use this number to determine if your rate is faster or slower than your normal. This is your unique baseline that will be essential to your understanding and success in using exercise as a method for stimulating the Vagus nerve.

The wonderful news is that you do not even need to invest in a tool like this to know your heart rate and your well-being. If a person you are encouraging to use exercise as a means for the stimulation of their Vagus nerve, you can encourage them to get a monitor and learn their own baseline, or you can encourage them to just use their common sense and pay attention to signs.

For example, did they get an injury for overuse of a muscle or joint? Are they having a major shift to their appetite? Are they more irritable? Having trouble sleeping? These are signs that exercise has passed healthy and is not extreme. These are signs that you need to adjust your exercise regimen or the person you are assisting needs to make some changes.

Conducting a Loving-Kindness Meditation to Help Lift the Mood and Connectivity

Connecting with others in a meaningful, "heart to heart" moment is an excellent way to improve your vagal tone and vagal tone of others. Barbara Fredrickson, from the University of North Carolina at Chapel Hill, is a researcher known for trailblazing the way for understanding the Vagus nerve. Think about a time when you and another person were "on the same page," and you felt a reciprocal connection. The hypothesis is that there is an "upward spiral" of stimulation when the feedback loop is multi-directional, leading to an increase in vagal tone. This loop of feedback can be engaged in at various places where it can start. And more and more research shows that people who enjoy a higher level of vagal tone also enjoy better health, less chronic inflammation, better social connections, and better regulation of emotions.

But these moments of connection do not need to occur in momentous conversations and interactions. These are best in small moments of connection between just two people. When this is a genuine and wholehearted connection, the parasympathetic response is triggered for both people. The psychological and visceral feedback is warm and peaceful. This leads to an expanded social connection, continuing to spread positivity and pro-social behavior. This is an incredible evolutionary aspect that is part of the natural human need for connection and nurturing. It develops a cooperative bond and something designed to support both harmony in oneself and in a collective situation.

The key to this increase in vagal tone and Vagus nerve stimulation lies in the expression of loving-kindness to others, and also to yourself. To do this, there are four key stages:

1. Offer thoughts of loving-kindness to loved ones, neighbors, family, and friends.
2. Offer loving-kindness to all people in the world experiencing struggle and discord.

3. Offer loving-kindness to people that have let you down in the past or have hurt you.
4. Finally, offer loving kindness to yourself, forgiving yourself for any harm or negativity you have caused to yourself or to other people.
5. It is important to note that you need to be in a relaxed state, even in meditation, to accomplish this effectively. You also need to extend this loving-kindness to yourself. If you do not feel worthy of forgiveness and compassion, you cannot expect to offer it genuinely to others.